Florida

FLORIDA BY ROAD

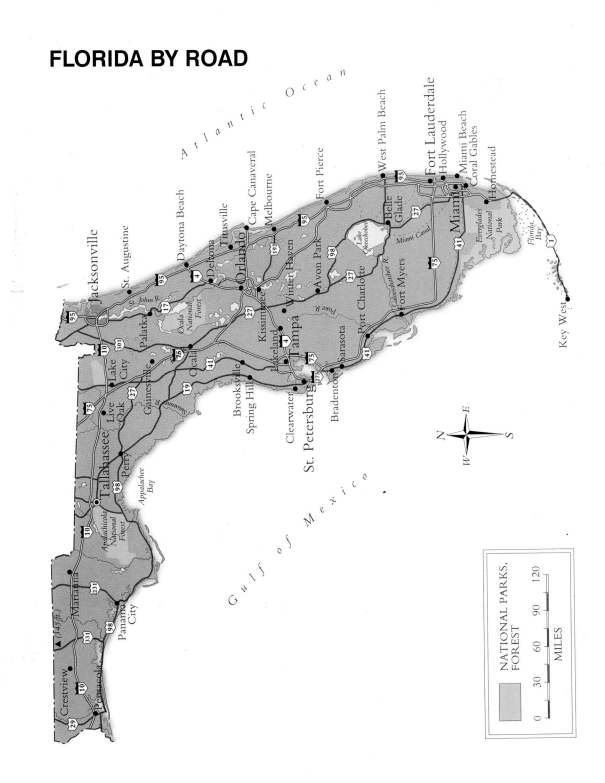

Atlantic Ocean

Jacksonville
St. Augustine
Daytona Beach
Deltona
Titusville
Cape Canaveral
Melbourne
Fort Pierce
West Palm Beach
Fort Lauderdale
Hollywood
Miami Beach
Coral Gables
Miami
Homestead

Orlando
Winter Haven
Avon Park
Belle Glade
Lake Okeechobee
Miami Canal
Everglades National Park
Florida Bay

St. Johns R.
Palatka
Ocala National Forest
Kissimmee
Lakeland
Tampa
Port Charlotte
Fort Myers
Caloosahatchee R.
Key West

Live Oak
Gainesville
Ocala
Brooksville
Spring Hill
Clearwater
St. Petersburg
Bradenton
Sarasota
Peace R.
Suwannee R.

Lake City
Tallahassee
Perry
Appalachee Bay
Apalachicola National Forest

Marianna
(345 ft.)
Panama City
Crestview
Pensacola

Gulf of Mexico

N E S W

NATIONAL PARKS, FOREST

MILES

0   30   60   90   120

Celebrate the States

Florida

Perry Chang and Joyce Hart

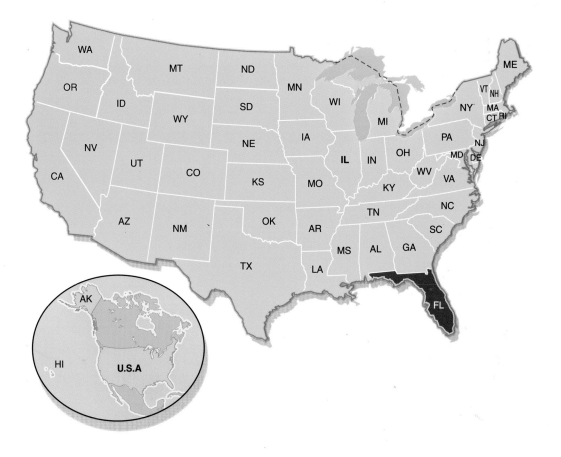

mc **Marshall Cavendish**
Benchmark
New York

Marshall Cavendish Benchmark
99 White Plains Road
Tarrytown, NY 10591-9001
www.marshallcavendish.us

Library of Congress Cataloging-in-Publication Data
Hart, Joyce, 1954–
Florida / by Joyce Hart and Perry Chang.—2nd ed.
p. cm. — (Celebrate the states)
Summary: "Provides comprehensive information on the geography, history, wildlife, governmental structure, economy, cultural diversity, peoples, religion, and landmarks of Florida"—Provided by publisher.
Includes bibliographical references and index.
ISBN-13: 978-0-7614-2348-5
ISBN-10: 0-7614-2348-6
1. Florida—Juvenile literature. I. Chang, Perry. II. Title. III. Series.
F311.3.H36 2007
975.9—dc22
2006008174

Editor: Christine Florie
Editorial Director: Michelle Bisson
Art Director: Anahid Hamparian
Series Designer: Adam Mietlowski

Photo research by Connie Gardner

Cover Photo: George Schaub/SuperStock

The photographs in this book are used by permission and courtesy of; *Corbis:* Bill Ross, back cover; Gavriel Jecan, 8; Farrell Grehan, 12; Stephen Frink, 15, 135; Carlos Barria, 21; Tony Arruza, 26; James L. Amos, 40; G.E. Kidder Smith, 43; Edwards, 45; Osborne, 46; Bettmann, 49; Catherine Karnow, 56; Jeffery Allan Salter, 58; Buddy Mays, 61; Douglas Peebles, 70; Reuters, 75, 127, 132; Kelly-Mooney Photography, 86; Mark M. Lawrence, 89; Karen Kasmauski, 98; Jonathan Blair, 103; David Muench, 104; Richard T. Nowitz, 105; Joseph Sohm, 109; Kevin Fleming, 111; Galen Rowell, 115; Arthur Morris, 117; Lynda Richardson, 118; Patrick Ward, 124; Corbis, 129. *Image Works:* A Avampini/V&W, 31; Jeff Greenberg, 53, 54, 67, 73, 101; David Frazier, 80, 82. *APWide World Photos:* AP Photo, 79. *PhotoEdit:* Dennis MacDonald, 113 (lower). *SuperStock:* Eric SA House-Carie, 10; R. Ashworth, 11; The Cummer Museum of Art and Gardens, Jacksonville, 31; Alan Briere, 107; Age Fotostock, 113 (top). *SilverImage:* 77. *The Granger Collection:* 35, 39, 41, 48, 130. *Alamy:* Bob Elsdale, 29; Jeff Greenberg, 64, 87, 96; Mark J. Barrett, 100. Bill Bachmann, 123. *Getty:* Tony Ranze, 19; Mark Wilson, 23; Hulton Archive, 32; National Geographic, 83; Joe Raedle, 84, 94; NASA, 91; Jonathan Ferrey, 133. *Dembinsky Photo Associates:* Barbara Gerlach, 17; Dominique Braud, 18. *North Wind Picture Archive:* 42.

Printed in China
135642

Contents

Florida is a beautiful place to live.

"It's got the good climate you need for all the water sports, plus tennis, swimming, running. It's kind of relaxing on the shore. It's pretty laid back, listening to the water, watching the sunset."

—government official Andrew Maurey

It was once a wild, lush frontier . . .

"Vast portions of the peninsula lay remote, forbidding, inaccessible, and unsettled."

—historians Raymond Mohl and Gary Mormino

. . . it is more settled now, but still remains beautiful.

"The Florida skies are like no other, with cloud formations that are awesome! Even when it rains the sun shines through the drops."

—stock broker Connie Letang

Many people come from other states to make Florida their home . . .

"I came from Michigan seven years ago, and every year I learn to love the winters in Florida even more."

—insurance executive Patrick Ehnis

"For a lot of people in different times in their life, Florida represents a new start."

—minister Larry Reimer

. . . and find something to love about Florida.

"There are only five bad weather days a year here in Florida, and they aren't even that bad!"

—retired professional golfer Dick Ptomey

"There's a kind of cosmopolitan mix, at least in larger cities, that I like— a real mix of people, with a little bit of southern gentility mixed in, that makes it a kinder, gentler place to live."

—minister Clarke Campbell-Evans

Florida is different things to different people. To some Florida is a paradise. It is warm water, sun-drenched beaches, mysterious swamps, and stunning coral reefs. To others it is the rural South. It is small towns, pickup trucks, and tomato fields. To still others it is a vacationland with high-rise hotels, amusement parks, and bumper-to-bumper traffic.

Florida is all of these things and much more. Jutting out several hundred miles from the continental United States toward the Caribbean, Florida is a cultural crossroads where people of different backgrounds have mingled, traded, and sometimes fought. This is Florida's story.

Chapter One

Dangerous and Endangered

Florida, as most Floridians know, is much more than palm trees and white sandy beaches. The long peninsular state, surrounded by the warm waters of the Gulf of Mexico and the Atlantic Ocean, is teeming with plants and animals that thrive in the gentle winters and hot, humid summers. Away from the waters of Florida's coastlines are thick forests in the north, wide swamps in the south, and lakes, big and small, in almost every area in between.

Florida is home to thousands of sun-loving residents, including humans and other mammals, fish and birds, reptiles, insects, and a glorious array of vegetation. All these elements don't always work together in harmony. But as time goes by, Floridians strive to make adjustments to keep the Sunshine State's environment healthy and productive.

WOODS AND WETLANDS

Florida is easily divided into two sections: the panhandle and the peninsula. Northwestern Florida, the narrow part of the state that hugs the Gulf Coast

To many, flamingoes symbolize Florida. They can be found throughout Florida's parks and wetlands.

south of Alabama and Georgia, is called the panhandle. The peninsula, a strip of land surrounded by water, extends about 400 miles into the water, separating the Gulf of Mexico from the Atlantic Ocean.

A chain of islands called the Florida Keys arcs out into the Gulf from the southern tip of the peninsula. The southernmost of these islands, Key West, lies just 90 miles from the island nation of Cuba.

Florida has three ecological regions: hardwood forests, pine barrens, and wetlands. Hardwood forests cover north Florida and sections of central Florida, the parts of the state with the highest elevation. The abundance of fertile soil in these areas nourishes forests of hardwood trees, such as beech, holly, hickory, magnolia, maple, and oak.

More than eight hundred keys off the tip of Florida span more than 106 miles into the Atlantic Ocean and Gulf of Mexico.

Pine barrens—areas of rugged pine forests—spread out over much of central Florida. There, the dry, sandy soil is less fertile than in northern Florida, so most hardwood trees are unable to grow. Instead, pine trees thrive, along with scrub oaks and palmettos.

A century ago a large portion of Florida lay underwater for at least part of the year. Today, the remaining swamps and marshland that make up the state's wetlands are concentrated in central and southern Florida. The Gulf Coast's saltwater marshes are an ideal habitat for mangrove trees, which have roots that thrust up out of the water. Also growing there are water lilies, cattails, saw grass, bay trees, and cypress trees.

At 729,000 acres, Big Cypress National Preserve has a diverse environment ranging from pines, mangrove forests, and cypress to white-tailed deer, Florida panthers, and bears.

The most famous stretch of Florida wetlands is the Everglades, a chain of lakes, rivers, and marshland that spread over much of southern Florida. Much of this vast wetland is made up of grasses growing up out of slow-moving water, and it is dotted with small tree islands called hummocks. "They are, they have always been, one of the unique regions of the earth, remote, never wholly known," wrote the early environmentalist Marjory Stoneman Douglas in her classic book *The Everglades: River of Grass*. "Nothing anywhere else is quite like them."

South-central Florida's Lake Okeechobee is one of the nation's largest lakes, smaller than only the Great Lakes and Utah's Great Salt Lake. It is the largest of the more than 30,000 freshwater lakes and ponds that are located in Florida.

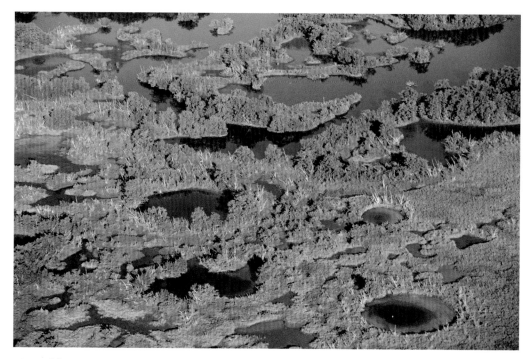

A World Heritage Site, Everglades National Park is North America's only subtropical preserve.

LAND AND WATER

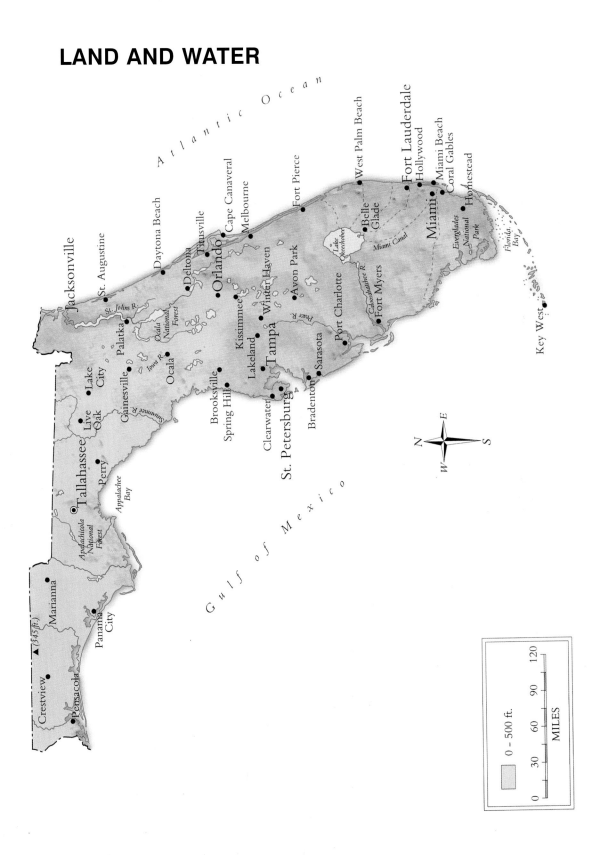

HOLES AND REEFS

Much of the United States sits on top of granite, slate, and marble—very solid and hard rock types. In Florida limestone lies underneath the ground. An ocean once covered Florida, and the remains of sea life helped to form the limestone. Limestone is a hard rock form, too, but water (especially if the water contains acids that have seeped in from the ground) can, and does, cut holes into the limestone. Over millions of years, the limestone under Florida has become filled with holes. This has allowed springs and rivers to form underground. This is good in some ways. For instance, the underground springs feed most of Florida's rivers and lakes. In other ways, however, this is not helpful.

Sometimes so many holes appear in the underground limestone that it caves in, forming deep depressions in the land called sinkholes. Sinkholes have been known to appear suddenly in roads, parking lots, and even in some people's backyards. Sinkholes sometimes reach as deep as 200 feet. Deep sinkholes often fill with water and become popular swimming holes. Many lakes in Florida actually sit atop sinkholes that are farther underground.

Lying underwater off the Florida coast is one of the state's most unusual geographic features—coral reefs. A coral reef is a limestone formation made up of the skeletons of millions of tiny sea creatures called polyps. Living polyps that attach to these limestone bases give coral reefs their beautiful colors and extraordinary shapes, which sometime resemble fans and branches. Brightly colored tropical fish often live among the reefs, creating an exotic and lively underwater world.

The coral reefs that hug the Atlantic coastline near Miami and then wind around the Florida Keys are the only natural reefs located off the continental United States. The warm Gulf Stream water flowing through the Straits of Florida, between the southern tip of Florida and Cuba, nourishes these reefs.

Florida's coral reefs formed five to seven thousand years ago. The reefs supply food, shelter, and breeding areas for the many plants and animals that live there.

Even after people appeared on the Florida peninsula some 12,000 years ago, huge, now-extinct animals such as woolly mammoths, mastodons, and giant tree sloths still lived there. Today, squirrels, raccoons, armadillos, opossums, deer, turtles, rabbits, otters, and gophers thrive inland. Florida panthers live primarily in the Everglades. Ordinary birds, such as blue jays, vultures, crows, woodpeckers, robins, owls, geese, cardinals, and mockingbirds, dot the state.

Florida also plays at least part-time host to a range of rarer birds, such as the lovely long-billed roseate spoonbill and the anhinga, which Floridians call the snakebird or water turkey. The anhinga puts its whole body, wings and all, into the water when it swims. Only its long curved neck and head stick out, which makes it look like a snake swimming in the water. After the bird leaves the water, it holds out its wings to dry them off. Otherwise, it would be too heavy to fly. This blow-drying pose makes the bird look like a turkey, giving rise to its other nickname.

Florida is home to many snakes that bite, but only coral snakes, certain rattlesnakes, and cottonmouths, which are also called water moccasins, are poisonous. Some of Florida's snakes help to keep the rodent population in check. Without the snakes, rats and mice would be a lot more abundant.

Florida's warm weather creates the perfect living conditions for many things, including a wide assortment of insects, such as mosquitoes, cockroaches, and fire ants. However distracting these insects can be to humans, they do well in keeping the birds and frogs well fed.

One of Florida's most famous creatures, the alligator, almost disappeared from the state. From the 1800s until the late 1960s, many Floridians hunted the alligator, mostly because they could sell its skin, which was then turned into leather used to make purses and boots. A decline in the alligator

An anhinga dries off in the Florida sun.

population caused this large reptile to be placed on the endangered species list in 1967. Ten years later the alligator population experienced a comeback and was moved to the threatened list. Then, in the 1990s, Florida's alligators faced another threat because they were being slowly poisoned by toxic waste in the water. Another threat to the alligator is loss of their natural habitat as wetlands are drained to create dry land on which to build houses, golf courses, and shopping malls.

Alligators are most visible when they are sunning themselves. These cold-blooded reptiles need to lie in the sun to raise their body temperature. Alligators grow to be up to 13 feet long. They have sharp teeth and powerful tails, and they can run very quickly on land for short distances.

Cold-blooded alligators are often seen sunning along the banks of ponds throughout Florida.

They have no natural enemies except for humans. State and environmental groups constantly monitor the large reptiles' habitat to keep Florida a good place for alligators to live.

HOT, WET, AND WINDY

Florida's plants and animals, as well as the state's human population, have had to adapt to the hot climate and sometimes unstable weather that occurs in this state. Most of Florida experiences two seasons. There is usually a very hot, humid summer and then a short, moderate winter. However, Florida's weather does not always follow this pattern. Some places in Florida do not have a winter at all. For instance, in the southern part of the state, the climate tends to be summerlike all year round. In contrast, the northern section has, on occasion, seen a little snow in the winter.

In southern Florida it is normal for winter to pass almost unnoticed. Often farmers can continue to grow and harvest fruits and vegetables throughout a typical winter. But sometimes even in the southern reaches of the state, temperatures dip below freezing. When this happens, large portions of the state's crops are wiped out.

Central Florida's climate is a little more moderate than the climate of the areas around Miami Beach and Key West, in the southern part of the state. In Tampa and Orlando, for instance, winter temperatures average about 60 degrees Fahrenheit. However, average temperatures only give you an idea of

In order to prevent crop damage, citrus growers spray water on their crops when temperatures drop below freezing. This provides some protection from the effects of freezing temperatures.

what is normal over a long time period. Central Florida is likely to also experience the effects of a blast of Arctic air during the winter, sending temperatures well below the freezing point for a couple of days. When Florida residents hear there is going to be a freeze, many of them wrap sheets and blankets around their outdoor garden plants and bring their pets inside to keep them warm. Oftentimes, this does not keep some of the more tender plants from turning completely black and then dying. Fortunately, the warm weather quickly returns, and the fertile soil welcomes new plants. By the summer, with temperatures in the 80s, central Florida gardens are in full bloom again.

North Florida has a more typical four-season year, with hardwood forests even featuring brightly colored leaves in the fall. Although it occasionally snows in northern Florida, winters are still rather short, and summers, like in all other parts of Florida, are hot and sticky. Although north Florida has achieved the state's lowest recorded temperature, –2 °F in Tallahassee in 1899, it has also suffered the state's highest temperature, 109 °F in Monticello in 1931.

High and low temperatures are one thing Floridians talk about when they discuss the weather. But the most discussed weather topic, especially in recent years, has been hurricanes. The year 2005 had the most active hurricane season in the 154 years that records have been kept. The official Atlantic hurricane season lasts between June 1 and November 30. This is the most likely time in which tropical storms will form in the warm moist air over the southern Atlantic Ocean, Caribbean Sea, Gulf of Mexico, and eastern Pacific Ocean. As they rotate in a counterclockwise direction around what is called the "eye of the storm," hurricanes gain strength. When a storm develops 74 mile-per-hour winds, it is officially upgraded from a tropical storm to a hurricane.

A Key West resident navigates a flooded street after Hurricane Wilma landed in October 2005.

In 2005 there were fourteen official hurricanes. Three of these storms reached Category 5 status, which means that at one time, the winds were blowing at a rate greater than 155 miles per hour. That is enough wind to blow a truck off the road, to take a roof off a house, and to topple huge oak trees. In both 2004 and 2005, four different hurricanes slammed into Florida and caused widespread damage to houses, trailer parks, office buildings, and roads. In addition to the high winds, hurricanes also drop a lot of rain and cause large waves to crash along the shore, eroding the beaches.

When hurricanes do not develop into dangerous Category 4 and 5 storms, some Floridians like the excitement the storms bring. They fill their bathtubs with water in case water pumps are shut down. They buy lots of candles and batteries for their flashlights in case electricity is turned off. They stock up on food that does not need to be cooked. Then they huddle in a safe room in the house and wait for the storm to blow over. Schools are usually closed, so students enjoy a day off, passing the time with old-fashioned activities like playing cards and board games that do not require electricity.

Thunderstorms are another kind of spectacular weather that Floridians experience. As a matter of fact, Florida is often referred to as the lightning capital of the world. The place in Florida that is most frequently hit with lightning bolts (in the whole United States) is a strip referred to as Lightning Alley, which runs from Tampa to Titusville. At the height of the thunderstorm season in August, Brevard County (where Titusville is located) is likely to experience over six thousand lightning strikes. The show of lightning in the skies over Florida can be as exciting to watch as a Fourth of July fireworks display. However, lightning heats the air around it to 50,000 °F, so the best thing for people to do when they hear thunder is to head indoors quickly. To determine how close the lightning is, some people start counting the seconds between hearing thunder and seeing the flash of lightning. Then they divide that number by five. That is how many miles the lightning is away. Whether near or far, though, the safest place for people to calculate this distance is inside.

During summer months, areas of Florida can sometimes experience a thunder and lightning storm once a day.

THE WEST PALM BEACH HURRICANE

In the days before weather satellites and the long-range tracking of hurricanes, these fierce tropical storms usually caught people by surprise. Despite modern advances in meteorology, the destructive force of hurricanes is still a reality as they sweep in every fall from the Caribbean. This song is as relevant today as it was when it was written in 1928.

On the six-teenth day of Sep-tem-ber, In nine-teen twen-ty eight, God start-ed rid-ing ear-ly, He rode 'til ve-ry late.

Chorus

In the storm, Oh, in the storm.— Lord, some-

bo - dy got drowned in the storm.

He rode out on the ocean
Chained the lightning to his wheel,
Stepped on land at West Palm Beach,
And the wicked hearts did yield.
Chorus

Over in Pahokee,
Families rushed out at the door,
And somebody's poor mother
Haven't been seen anymore.
Chorus

Some mothers looked at their children,
As they began to dry,
Cried, "Lord, have mercy,
For we all must die."
Chorus

I tell you wicked people,
What you had better do;
Go down and get the Holy Ghost
And then you live the life, too.
Chorus

Out around Okeechobee,
All scattered on the ground,
The last account of the dead they had
Were twenty-two hundred found.
Chorus

South Bay, Belle Glade, and Pahokee,
Tell me they all went down,
And over at Chosen,
Everybody got drowned.
Chorus

Some people are yet missing,
And they haven't been found, they say.
But this we know, they will come forth
On the Resurrection Day.
Chorus

When Gabriel sounds the trumpet,
and the dead begin to rise,
I'll met the saints from Chosen,
Up in the heavenly skies.
Chorus

As beautiful, varied, and dangerous as Florida's environment can be, it is also vulnerable. The state, once an unspoiled subtropical paradise, has quickly acquired more than its share of environmental problems. Rapid population growth is primarily to blame for these issues.

The catastrophic effects of the state's ever-increasing population are most evident in south Florida. There, human intervention now threatens the very existence of the Everglades.

Until the twentieth century, water from central Florida flowed southward into the Kissimmee River, Lake Okeechobee, and then through the Everglades into Florida Bay at the southern tip of the peninsula. In the 1960s the government eliminated the bends in the Kissimmee River, turning it into a straight-line ditch. They built a 100-mile-long dike around Lake Okeechobee, as well as canals from

The U.S. Army Corp of Engineers and the South Florida Water Management District regulate Lake Okeechobee's water via canals, dikes, and floodgates.

the lake to the area's rivers. As a result water that used to flow slowly south through the Everglades into Florida Bay now flows either directly east into the Atlantic or west into the Gulf of Mexico. This drained the area south of the lake, turning it into some of the world's richest agricultural land. Draining these wetlands also made room for suburban development in the area.

It is now clear that the authorities did too good a job of drying out the Everglades. Rainwater flows so quickly to the Atlantic and the Gulf today that little remains for the slow flow southward. As a result, the Everglades dry out more than ever during the dry season. This means that wildfires rage more frequently in the wintertime, and that fragile native plants are being crowded out by hardier plants from other parts of the world, which are better able to survive the dry conditions. South Florida, historically one of the wettest areas of the country, now suffers from water shortages.

Scientists have discovered that wetlands and winding rivers such as the Kissimmee help the environment because they curb flooding and purify water naturally. Work has begun on an effort to undo what was done to the Kissimmee River in the 1960s. Some of this work includes re-creating the bends in the river that used to occur naturally. To do this, engineers are building the banks of the river back up, forcing the water to snake around as it did before. However, the hurricanes that have hit Florida in the past years have undone some of that work to restore the river's natural shape.

The farms and housing developments that were built on the dried land caused other problems as well. Pesticides are being spread throughout the area in an effort to kill insects and thus protect the people who live there as well as the crops that are cultivated in this area. Scientists fear that these pesticides will eventually enter Florida's underground water supply, killing fish and threatening the quality of the state's drinking water.

UNINVITED GUESTS

As if Florida's Everglades were not having enough problems, there are now exotic creatures showing up from other countries, threatening the already threatened species. Consider, for example, the Burmese python (right), which can grow to be as big as 20 feet long. Sightings of these huge snakes are becoming more common. About seventy of these snakes have been caught by local park rangers in the past decade, and it is estimated that there are still plenty more of them living in the wild. Battles between alligators and pythons can be riveting to watch, as some tourists have discovered, but the pythons are gobbling up many of the smaller animals that live in the wetlands. The big snakes eat everything from squirrels and rats to birds, competing with smaller snakes, such as the eastern indigo snake, a reptile that is on Florida's threatened species list.

Other non-native creatures have also appeared in Florida. There are monkeys living in woods where no monkeys ever lived before, such as in Dania Beach, not far from Miami. Non-native fish are also showing up in Florida's waters. In addition, new plants have been introduced from other parts of the world.

Non-native species are often brought into the area by people who buy exotic plants and animals for their homes. When the plants or animals become a nuisance (or in the case of the pythons, become a danger), their owners often take them to the Everglades or some other uninhabited (by humans) place and dump them. This can be devastating to the native populations of vegetation and animal life. Some exotic plants are invasive—they grow fast and take over an entire area, smothering all the native plants. This causes a breakdown in the biodiversity of that environment. Instead of many different plants growing in one area, one plant dominates.

In the case of animal life, such as the battle between the alligators and the pythons, so far the alligators are holding their ground. They have been seen with pythons in their large jaws. However, as the population of these snakes expands, no one knows for sure who will win the fight.

Another cause for environmental concern is the fertilizer used in farming and on lawns. Farmers feed cattle phosphorus as a nutrient. When cow manure laced with phosphorus settles in lakes, however, it can speed the growth of algae, which can choke lakes. This is happening in Lake Okeechobee. When the algae die and then decay, the oxygen in the water is used up. Fish and other wildlife die. Although Floridians are becoming more aware of the possible death of Lake Okeechobee, the battle is nowhere close to being over. Phosphorus levels have been lowered, but many environmentalists claim they are not low enough to save the lake.

PROTECTING THE ENVIRONMENT AND PRESERVING THE STATE

In 1999 the Florida legislature signed a bill that created the Florida Forever Program. The program provided up to $3 billion to help buy environmentally sensitive areas, to restore waterways, and to preserve important historical and cultural sites and is in effect until 2010. In the first five years of the program, it helped to preserve 1.25 million acres of land. This makes the Florida Forever Program one of the world's largest land-buying conservation programs.

Since the beginning of this program, the habitats of 190 rare and endangered plants and animals have been protected by the state. The lands that have been purchased include fragile coastline property, ecological greenways, natural floodplains, important lakes, and sustainable forests. Also included in the land purchases are archaeological and historical sites, such as the Letchworth Mounds State Park, which contains an ancient Native-American ceremonial site, located east of Tallahassee. Another purchase of over 16,000 acres of land on the Yellow River in northern Florida will restore the natural habitat and protect the rare and endangered plants and animals that live in those wetlands.

THE GENTLE GIANT

Of all the creatures threatened by the development of Florida's wet-lands, the most beloved is the West Indian manatee. Although it has been estimated that at least 1,435 manatees live in Florida's waters, 2005 saw the largest number of deaths of these lovable creatures, with almost 400 of them killed by boats or by swallowing fishing gear, or dying of natural or unknown causes.

The manatees' habitat is continually shrinking because of drainage and development. These huge, slow-moving mammals eat as much as 100 pounds of plants each day and sometimes weigh 3,500 pounds. Boats pose the most immediate danger to the animals. Because manatees are slow and must surface to breathe, motorboats speeding through the water often hit them or cut them with their propellers. As a result propeller marks frequently scar the manatees' gray, leathery skin. "They're big, cuddly, dumb animals that are really innocently getting slaughtered," said Greg Diehl, who once worked for Florida's manatee protection program.

The manner of their fishing.

A Cannow

Chapter Two

Becoming Florida

The first Floridians, sometimes referred to as Florida's First People or Native Americans from the Archaic period, made their way to the region roughly 12,000 years ago. The First People migrated from place to place as they searched for food. Some of the people hunted animals on the land, others caught fish, and still others collected fruits and berries that grew naturally. The area that would eventually become Florida was a lot different 12,000 years ago than it is today. The weather was cooler and drier. There were deer back then, as well as turtles, raccoons, and rattlesnakes. There were also mastodons and mammoths, which are large prehistoric animals.

Thousands of years later the descendants of the First People began to settle down a little more. New sources of food had appeared, such as alligators, squirrels, frogs, and aquatic birds. By 3,000 years ago there was more moisture in the air, temperatures began to rise, and small villages began to appear. By 1000 C.E., there were chiefs who ruled good-sized towns, and corn, beans, and squash were being grown in community gardens in some parts of what would become Florida. Remnants of these towns have been

The Seminole depended largely on hunting and fishing, as well as crops from gardening, for food.

uncovered, for example, in what is now the Tampa Bay area. Then, by 700 C.E., burial mounds were created, as was pottery and woven baskets. This is about the time that mosquitoes also made an appearance.

Other groups, such as those that lived along the Saint Johns and Indian rivers, had not yet developed any form of agriculture but rather continued to gather wild plants for food.

NATIVE-AMERICAN LIFE

Many different Native-American people lived in what would eventually become Florida. Some of the largest groups included the Ais, who lived on the eastern shore of the peninsula; the Apalachee, who lived in the north around present-day Tallahassee; the Calusa, who lived around present-day Tampa; the Chatot, who lived to the west of the Apalachicola River; the Pensacola, who lived in the Pensacola Bay area; the Seminole, who lived in various locations through the whole peninsula, possibly as far south as present-day Miami; the Tequesta people, who lived in what would later become Miami; and the Timucua (or Utina), who spread out between the Suwannee and Saint Johns rivers. There were many more smaller groups as well as groups so large that they spread across Georgia or parts of Alabama and Louisiana and then into the northern portions of the Florida peninsula.

Although all these different peoples spoke unique languages and often clashed with one another, they shared some common lifestyles and customs. Many of the Native-American groups were ruled by chieftains and religious leaders. Several of the villages were arranged around a chieftain's house and council buildings, in which meetings took place. Many of the houses were made from small branches woven together and then covered with mud and clay. The roofs of these houses were thatched with palm leaves.

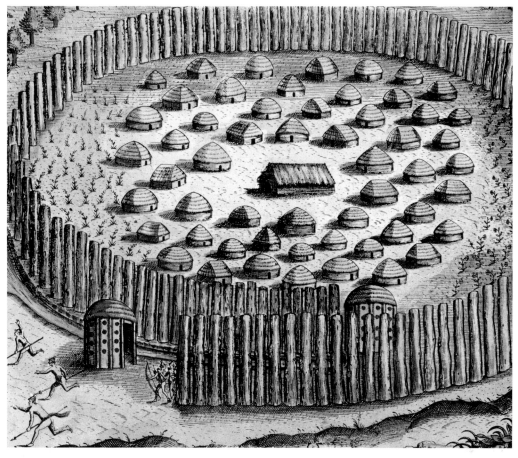

A colored engraving depicts an Indian village with its council house at its center.

One group, the Timucua, knew about a special plant called the yaupon holly, which when roasted and then added to water, made a drink that was similar in some ways to coffee. The drink made people sweat or even vomit, leading the Timucua people to believe that by drinking the so-called Black Drink, their spirits and bodies would be purified. The caffeine in the holly leaves gave them a boost of energy, so the Black Drink was often consumed by warriors before they went into battle.

The Timucua people traded the holly leaves with other tribes for materials they did not have, such as stones for making arrowheads.

These early peoples relied on oral histories, tales about their history passed from generation to generation through storytelling, to keep information. Most of the early accounts of Native Americans and their leaders in written form, therefore, were recorded by European invaders and settlers or gleaned from evidence that archaeologists have dug up at the sites of ancient villages and burial grounds.

THE ARRIVAL OF THE EUROPEANS

Spanish explorers were the first Europeans to make contact with Florida's Native Americans. A fleet sailing from Puerto Rico under Juan Ponce de León landed in Florida in 1513. Either because of the land's flowery appearance or because he landed around Easter, which was known as *Pascua Florida,* or "feast of the flowers," Ponce de León dubbed the peninsula "La Florida." Ponce de León and a series of other Spanish expeditions led by Pánfilo de Narváez, Hernando de Soto, and Pedro Menéndez de Avilés were looking for precious metals, such as gold. In the process they also tried to conquer the land and its people.

During winter 1521, Ponce de León made his second trip to Florida in order to establish a permanent colony. The group was ambushed by the Calusa tribe and the settlement was abandoned.

Álvar Núñez Cabeza de Vaca was one of four survivors of an ill-fated Spanish expedition into Florida. In July 1528, after looting the grain supply of Native Americans in north Florida, the expedition headed for Apalachicola Bay. In his classic account of the journey, Cabeza de Vaca wrote admiringly of the Native-Americans skills with bow and arrows:

Good armor did no good against arrows in this skirmish. There were men who swore they had seen two red oaks, each the thickness of a man's calf, pierced from side to side by arrows this day; which is no wonder when you consider the power and skill the Indians can deliver them with. I myself saw an arrow buried half a foot in a poplar tree.

All the Indians we had so far seen in Florida had been archers. They loomed big and naked and from a distance looked like giants. They were handsomely proportioned, lean, agile, and strong. Their bows were as thick as an arm, six or seven feet long, accurate at twenty paces.

Thanks to Florida's rough environment and the Spaniards' supply problems and weakening empire back in Europe, all these expeditions failed. In 1565 Menéndez, however, did establish a settlement at Saint Augustine in northeast Florida. This is the oldest permanent European settlement in the United States.

In the long run the arrival of the Spanish devastated the Native-American population for reasons that had nothing to do with warfare. Travel had exposed Europeans to most of the world's diseases.

Don Pedro Menéndez de Avilés landed off the coast of Florida on August 28, 1565, the Feast of Saint Augustine. Eleven days later, he and his soldiers fortified a Timucuan village and renamed it Saint Augustine.

But the isolated Native Americans had never faced many of the diseases the Europeans brought with them to the Americas, so their immune systems had no natural resistance to them. Florida's Native-American population dropped from 350,000 to 1,000 in the two centuries following Ponce de León's arrival. "Their whole social structure was completely uprooted by disease," said the historian David Proctor.

Disease was not the only reason the Native American population decreased. Soon after the first explorers landed in Florida, Spanish priests came to the region to try to convert the Native Americans to Christianity. Sometimes the Native Americans were killed if they refused to change their beliefs. The Native Americans already had well-developed spiritual beliefs based on their own gods.

However, it was often the case that many of the Native Americans, who were already ravaged by the European diseases and impressed by the Spaniards' military might, eventually invited Spanish priests to live among them in their villages. Many Native Americans converted to Catholicism, at least outwardly. Eventually, several dozen Spanish missions dotted the north Florida landscape.

In addition to Native Americans and Spaniards, Florida was home to many African Americans.

Spanish priests arrived in Florida to convert the Native Americans to the teachings of Christianity.

The Spanish brought Africans to Florida as slaves. Many free blacks, some of whom had escaped slavery in other colonies, also lived in the area. Compared with other parts of what would become the United States, Spanish Florida developed a less rigid attitude toward racial separation. Intermarriage, or at least interracial child-bearing, among Spaniards, Native Americans, and African Americans was common.

This relatively peaceful society lasted less than a century before being destroyed by people from the north. The British were colonizing Georgia, and they eventually joined forces with the Creek, a Native-American group in that area, and began pressing south to Florida.

The Spaniards had built an impressive fort, the Castillo de San Marcos, at their Saint Augustine headquarters. It was made of a stone formed from seashells, a substance that the Spanish dubbed coquina (pronounced koh-KEE-nah). Twice in the early 1700s the British attacked Saint Augustine. The Spaniards and their Native-American and African-American allies survived these assaults because the coquina was so soft that the fort's thick walls absorbed British cannonballs without crumbling.

Some of the Creek continued to move into Florida to get away from troubles they were having in lands to the north. These Native Americans were in search of land on which to grow their plants. The Spanish settlers in Florida encouraged this migration of the Creek, as they believed the Native Americans living in the northern part of Florida would help to keep the

The Castillo de San Marcos was officially declared "complete" in 1695 after twenty-three years of construction.

British from entering. It was during this time, in the 1700s, that many of the Native-American groups became collectively referred to as the Seminoles, even though they belonged to several different tribes, including the Creek. Many of the white settlers in Florida did not approve of the Native Americans claiming any of the land, and a series of wars soon followed between the settlers, who were later supported by the U.S. government, and the Seminoles.

THE RISE OF ANDREW JACKSON

Although Native Americans were supported by the Spanish in their attempt to settle much of Florida, Spain eventually lost control of the region. "Vast swaths of Florida were totally unpoliced by any authority," said the historian David Proctor. From the mid-1780s on some African Americans fleeing slavery in Georgia and Alabama began living with Florida's Native Americans, becoming black Seminoles. Meanwhile, white Georgians, eyeing Florida lands, engaged in a series of skirmishes with the Native Americans and African Americans already living in Florida. These battles eventually gave rise to the First Seminole War.

The commander of U.S. troops in the First Seminole War was General Andrew Jackson. Throughout his career in Florida, Jackson ruthlessly pursued his goal of removing all the Native Americans (those he did not kill) to lands west of Florida.

In 1818 General Andrew Jackson led troops into Florida in the First Seminole War, helping the United States acquire the region.

After defeating the Seminoles and with the passage of the Removal Act of 1830, the U.S. government tried to relocate all the Florida Seminoles to Indian Territory, in what would later become the state of Oklahoma. This attempt, however, lead to the Second Seminole War, as many of the Seminoles fiercely protected their right to stay in Florida.

The Seminoles won several early battles in the Second Seminole War (1835–1842), led by Osceola, who promised that he and his men would fight until the last drop of their blood moistened the ground. The U.S. troops became increasingly frustrated by the Seminole victories, and so they set a trap. In 1837 they lured the Seminoles, including Osceola, to a meeting by promising them a peace treaty. The U.S. government had no intention of offering the treaty and instead captured Osceola and most of his warriors.

This woodcut depicts the capture of Seminole chiefs by U.S. troops during the Second Seminole War.

Osceola died in prison a year later, in 1838. Twenty years later, in 1858, the last of the Seminole Wars ended in Palm Beach County, and most of the Native Americans were forced to leave. All but a few hundred Seminoles refused to go. Instead they headed for the Everglades, where they hid for several decades, not venturing out until the turn of the twentieth century.

STATEHOOD AND THE CIVIL WAR

In 1839 Floridians wrote their first state constitution and submitted it to the U.S. Congress in an attempt to gain statehood. By this time, as far as the white settlers were concerned, most, if not all, the Native Americans had disappeared, and many of the African Americans living in the area had been forced back into slavery. These facts encouraged more white people to descend on the new U.S. territory. Some of them were wealthy planters from Georgia and the Carolinas who moved south with their families and slaves. They began growing cotton in the five-county area around Tallahassee, the new territorial capital. This region soon began to look like the Old South, with its cotton fields, large estates, plantation houses, and black-majority populations. Because of the nearby bend around the Gulf of Mexico, this cotton plantation area became known as the Big Bend.

Large plantation houses dominated Big Bend, while pioneer farmers (above) located to other areas to grow crops and hunt.

Poorer white families moved into the rest of north Florida. These hardy pioneers raised beef cattle, tapped pine trees for turpentine, chopped down trees to sell to timber mills, trapped raccoons for their fur, and hunted, fished, and grew vegetables for food. Some found the rugged lifestyle too difficult and returned north or moved out west. Others stuck with it. "The main thing was to live their own lives, to live off the land," said the librarian Frank Mendola.

The population had grown to over 50,000 people, with African-American slaves making up almost half of that number. Political and economic power at this time was held by the plantation owners in central Florida, who were successful in getting Florida admitted as a slave state in March 1845. At that time states were being categorized as either free states or slave states, with Northerners and Southerners attempting to keep a balance of states on either side of the slavery issue. For instance, when Florida was accepted as a slave state, Iowa was admitted the next year as a free state. However, things were about to change, as Abraham Lincoln came into office, determined to end slavery once and for all.

In 1861 Floridians seceded from the Union and allied with other Southern states to join the Confederacy. White Floridians were determined to defend their right to own slaves. Although Florida was not actually the scene of major fighting during the Civil War, the people of Florida supplied salt, beef, and about 15,000 soldiers to what would become the losing effort of the Confederacy. Another two thousand Floridians, both white and black, joined the Northern, or the Union, army.

After the Civil War, Florida did not have to rebuild its cities, as none had suffered any destruction. Instead, Florida's harbors became busy with shipping lumber and other construction supplies to the devastated cities in the other Southern states that had taken the brunt of the fighting.

Confederate soldiers line up on the parade ground of Fort McRee, built between 1834 and 1839 to defend Pensacola and its harbor.

According to the law, slaves were freed, and many of them became share-croppers on the vast plantations in central Florida.

Despite the fact that slavery had been abolished, African Americans in Florida continued to suffer hardships. In the two decades following the Civil War, Florida legislators passed laws making it impossible for blacks to participate in government or to mingle as equals with whites. Laws required each adult, black or white, who wanted to vote to pay a tax. This tax was too costly for most African Americans. Therefore, they could not vote.

The Democratic Party soon dominated Florida politics, and Democrats banned blacks from the all-important Democratic primary, through which most elections were settled. By the turn of the twentieth century, laws had been established that kept blacks and whites from marrying each other, attending school together, or even sitting on buses together. Southern social customs kept blacks and whites from dining together or from merely shaking hands. This separation of blacks and whites was known as segregation.

Segregation kept many African Americans living in terror and poverty. A few, however, learned how to make the most of the situation. Because blacks could not eat in the same restaurants as whites or shop in the same

During segregation, Florida's African Americans were ordered to shop and eat in black-only establishments.

stores, some African Americans started their own restaurants and businesses. Soon, many Florida cities had thriving black business districts. Miami's black neighborhood of Overtown, for instance, featured an entertainment district that became known as Little Broadway. In the 1920s and 1930s the African-American pioneers of jazz and blues often stayed and performed there. Around this same time in northern Florida on Amelia Island, Abraham Lincoln Lewis, president of an African-American insurance company, founded American Beach, one of the few places along the Atlantic shoreline where African Americans could enjoy themselves at the ocean.

POPULATION GROWTH: 1830–2000

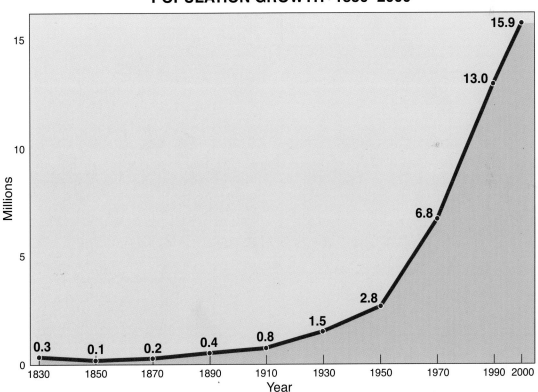

TOURISM AND THE REAL ESTATE BOOM

Many Floridian leaders at the turn of the twentieth century were busy working with northern businessmen to support Florida's economic growth. Northerners Henry Flagler and Henry Plant, for example, built railroads and beautiful hotels up and down the state. Frequently, the same trains that brought tourists into the state carried Florida's citrus fruit, an increasingly important farm product, out of the state to northern cities.

Promoters marketing the state as a tourist and retirement destination helped spur a massive real estate boom in south Florida in the 1920s. Up north, people heard about the fabulous money they could make by buying cheap Florida property and then reselling it at a higher price. As an example of how people were making money doing this, in 1925 two men

Miami exploded with new construction during the real estate boom in 1920s Florida.

bought a stretch of beach near Miami for $3 million and sold it two days later for $7.5 million. A week later it was sold again for $42 million. This kind of news spread fast, and soon people streamed down the Dixie Highway into Florida in order to get in on the action. Not all land deals were legitimate, though. Some businessmen who lacked moral principles sold swampland to unsuspecting northerners, forgetting to inform them that there was so much water on the land, they could not build any structures.

By 1926 the real estate madness had subsided. Land prices fell, and many people lost a lot of money. A devastating hurricane in September killed nearly four hundred people, a great number at that time. Two years later another hurricane hit, killing even more, about two thousand people. In 1929 the Great Depression descended on the entire country when the stock market crashed. People lost their jobs and had to stand in long lines to receive supplies of food from the government. There was no question at the time that the boom was over, at least for a while.

By the 1950s tourism had really taken hold in Florida. Attractions such as central Florida's Cypress Gardens and northeast Florida's Marineland, a forerunner of Sea World, led the way. Entertainers broadcast television shows from Miami Beach, which helped attract tourists to southern Florida. Northern college students began spending spring break on the Fort Lauderdale beaches and later on Daytona Beach and Panama City Beach.

During the 1950s, the beaches of coastal Florida became popular getaways for young college students.

THE CIVIL RIGHTS MOVEMENT IN FLORIDA

Although Florida was becoming increasingly prosperous and populated in the first half of the twentieth century, blacks still suffered widespread discrimination. Beginning in the late 1940s, Harry T. Moore, along with his wife Harriette, both of Mims, led a movement in the state to register African Americans to vote. They established the Brevard County branch of the National Association for the Advancement of Colored People and encouraged black teachers to sue the state for salaries equal to those of white teachers. Moore's work, unfortunately, did not escape the attention of white racists, people who did not like blacks and did not want to see African Americans succeed. On Christmas night, 1951, whites placed a bomb under the Moore's central Florida home. When it exploded, Harry and Harriette were both killed. The voter-registration effort spearheaded by the Moores, however, was successful enough that by 1960 a higher proportion of blacks were registered to vote in Florida than in all but one other state.

In the late 1950s and early 1960s Floridians, like people throughout the South, were trying to desegregate buses, restaurants, and motels. In Tallahassee in 1956, two African-American college students were arrested for sitting in a whites-only section of a bus. A young black minister, C. K. Steele, led a boycott of the bus company and became part of the influential national network of civil rights leaders associated with Dr. Martin Luther King Jr.

In 1964 civil rights activists threatened Florida's tourist industry by trying to desegregate public beaches, swimming pools, and motels. They targeted Saint Augustine in the midst of its celebration of the three hundredth anniversary of the Spanish settlement of the city. As blacks descended on the whites-only beaches and pools, white civil rights foes also crowded the city. State officials failed to keep the peace, and the headlines about violence at the Saint Augustine "swim-ins" helped push the U.S. Congress to pass the Civil Rights Act of 1964, which banned discrimination at public accommodations.

RISE OF TECHNOLOGY

By 1940 Florida was still the most sparsely populated southern state and only the twenty-seventh most populous state in the country. In fifty short years, however, it became the South's most urban and the nation's fourth most populous state. This was possible because of the rise of several technologies that made it easier to live year-round in central and south Florida.

In the 1840s the north Florida doctor John Gorrie, a former mayor of Apalachicola, had invented the basic technology for air conditioning and refrigeration as a way to treat his malaria patients, who ran high fevers. Later innovators perfected the technology. Air conditioning became widely available in the 1950s. First it was used to cool movie theaters, then other public buildings, and finally private homes. By the 1970s most middle-class Floridians could move from their air-conditioned homes to their air-conditioned cars to their air-conditioned offices, often without breaking into a sweat, even in 99 °F heat.

Other technologies also fueled the state's growth. Drainage and insect control technologies made the state a more comfortable place to live. The development of inexpensive cars made it possible for middle-class families to visit Florida as tourists. Airplanes made it easier for people from around the world to visit Florida. Both trucks and planes sped the delivery of Florida farm products to distant markets.

MOVING INTO THE TWENTY-FIRST CENTURY

Florida grabbed the attention of not only the residents of the other U.S. states but also of the world shortly after the twenty-first century rolled in.

The presidential election of 2000 between Democrat Al Gore and Republican George W. Bush was so close that Florida became a pivotal state in determining who would become the next U.S. president. Unfortunately, Florida's voting machines and ballots caused a lot of problems, and the nation had to wait for the courts, including the U.S. Supreme Court, to decide which candidate actually had won the presidency. With Florida's weakness in its voting procedures fully exposed to the world, the state began a massive program to rehabilitate and modernize its voting machines so the same problems would not happen again.

Politics was not the only area that received attention in Florida, however, as its fast-growing population and a seemingly unending procession of hurricanes slammed into the state in 2004 and 2005, applying pressure to the state's resources. But not all the news was so cloudy.

Florida was considered one of the world's top travel destinations, with more than 76 million visits recorded in 2005. The weather; the beaches; the tourist attractions, such as Walt Disney World and Universal Studios in Orlando and Busch Gardens in Tampa; the natural environment and state parks; the space program; and the professional sports teams continued to attract tourists. This fed the economy and promoted the growth and construction of the state's colleges and universities, among other things, as well as the transportation system, which in turn attracted more people to the state.

It was not just individuals who were attracted to Florida, though. More and more businesses, wanting to get away from higher taxes and lower temperatures in the northern states, were choosing Florida for their corporate headquarters. Because of this growth, in 2005 Florida held its place as the fourth most populated state, behind New York, California, and Texas.

With an estimated one thousand people moving to Florida each day of the year in 2005, the construction industry was booming, trying to build houses, apartments, and schools to handle all the new residents. New housing developments, however, meant that more water was pumped out of Florida's water reserves; more traffic was backed up on the highways; more pollutants were entering the air; and more land was taken away from the natural habitat of the other residents of the state—the plants and animals.

In recent years, Florida has been experiencing a heavy influx of retirees and young families seeking a lower cost of living. This has sparked new housing developments throughout the state.

Many Floridians are working together with businesses and scientists in attempts to keep the environment healthy. As they say at the Florida Department of Environmental Protection, "Florida's environmental priorities include restoring America's Everglades; improving air quality; restoring and protecting the water quality in our springs, lakes, rivers and coastal waters; conserving environmentally sensitive lands; and providing citizens and visitors with recreational opportunities, now and in the future." That is a big task that will require the cooperation of all Florida enthusiasts, including visitors, tourists, businesses, and residents.

Chapter Three

Cultural Crossroads

Florida is made up of people from all over the world, giving the state a rich diversity of cultures. It has the third largest immigration population in the United States; the Florida census now indicates that for every eight residents in the state, one of those was born in a country other than the United States.

Many people believe this rapid growth in population and cultural diversity is a very good thing for Florida. The cultural mix helps Floridians learn and appreciate other ways of living. However, there are some Floridians who do not agree. They are concerned that differences between people can cause many distracting disagreements. The debate will probably continue for a long time. In the meantime, the diversity of Florida's population brings to the state an interesting mix of opportunities and experiences.

Most of the immigrants to Florida come from the Caribbean and Latin America, including Cuba, Mexico, and other countries in Central and South America. Smaller but increasing numbers come from Asian countries, such as the Philippines, China, Vietnam, Korea, and India. Miami-Dade County receives the majority of immigrants, but counties up and down both the eastern and the western coastlines, as well as the Orlando area, attract immigrant populations, too.

Young Floridians share lemonade while enjoying the Jamaican Jerk Festival in Pembroke Pines.

Immigrating populations have been coming to Florida for a long time. Northern immigrants began arriving in Florida after the Civil War. By the turn of the twentieth century, the nation's wealthy elite were flooding into southeast Florida, the so-called Gold Coast. Some of the richest families in the country still live in Palm Beach and Boca Raton and across the peninsula in Naples.

In recent decades older people of all different backgrounds have moved from the Northeast and Midwest to central and south Florida, turning the state into a retirement haven. Many retirees return north

Florida's active retirement community takes advantage of the climate and surroundings of Florida.

for half the year, avoiding Florida's hot summers. Floridians call these folks "snowbirds." Native white Floridians have often had mixed feelings about these Northern migrants.

AFRICAN AMERICANS IN FLORIDA

Civil rights struggles gripped Florida in the 1950s and 1960s. Although some of these struggles come to the surface from time to time, there have been great strides made in recent years toward bridging the gaps. Dialogues between representatives from black neighborhoods and their white counterparts, for instance, have begun in various communities to make sure that problems of each group are understood. There is also a growing number of neighborhoods that host festivals celebrating the foods, arts, and entertainment of other nations in an effort to allow groups to better understand one another. For example, in Hallandale Beach, in south Florida, a community-relations committee was formed to bring a predominately white neighborhood together with one that was predominately black. This is not always an easy task, however. John Hardwick, a local barber and member of the committee board, said, "This board has a wonderful opportunity to bring about some true community relations. We've spent time trying to get to know each other and learn the lives of different people."

Improving community relations is one way to ease the tension between different groups of people. But allowing people to earn a fair wage and giving them good job opportunities is another way. Per capita income for Florida's blacks has, for a long time, been less than half that of whites. The unemployment rate among blacks in 2004 was almost three times that of white Floridians, and in 2005, the number of black families living in poverty was three times that of whites.

Nevertheless, life for many of the 15 percent of Floridians who are African American has improved in recent decades. Today, most Florida cities are less segregated than they were in the past. One in seven blacks employed in Florida works in a professional or managerial job. The gap between black and white infant mortality rates and black and white high school students' scores on standardized tests is slowly shrinking.

African Americans have also gradually made headway in Florida's business and political worlds. Since 1993, four African-American Floridians have been elected to the U.S. Congress, marking the first time since the years immediately following the Civil War (1866–1877) that blacks have represented Florida in Washington.

Sharon-Ames Dennard, 2002 Working Mother of the Year, reads to children in Tallahassee.

ETHNIC FLORIDA

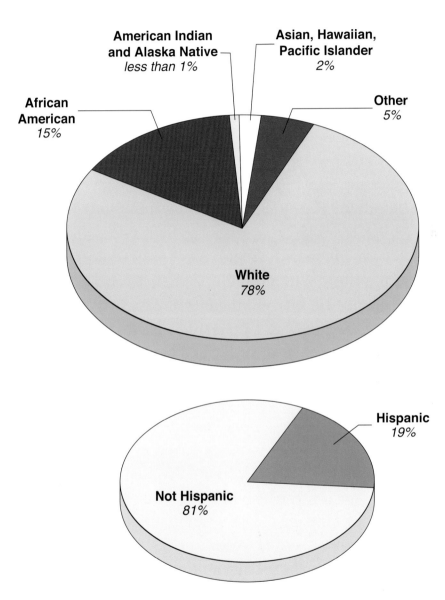

American Indian and Alaska Native *less than 1%*

Asian, Hawaiian, Pacific Islander *2%*

African American *15%*

Other *5%*

White *78%*

Hispanic *19%*

Not Hispanic *81%*

Note: A person of Cuban, Mexican, Puerto Rican, South or Central American, or other Spanish culture or origin, regardless of race, is defined as Hispanic.

Both Tampa and Miami have Cuban influences, but the mix of ethnic backgrounds does not stop there.

In the late 1800s Vicente Martinez Ybor created a cigar industry in the Tampa area. Over the years he brought over 12,000 fellow Cubans to the area to help him produce his special cigars. The community grew, and the Tampa area enjoyed a strong and growing Latin influence, as well as a reputation for making some very good cigars. Today, Tampa enjoys a strong Hispanic presence, as 10 percent of its population has roots in Mexico, Central and South America, and other Latin countries to the south.

Florida's other strongly Hispanic community lives in and around Miami. In 1959 a revolutionary army led by Fidel Castro seized power in Cuba. Castro's political foes and many professionals and business-people fled the island nation. Many of these Cuban exiles eventually settled in Miami. To survive, these well-educated immigrants frequently had to take jobs as waiters and taxi drivers, but only temporarily. They soon opened stores and restaurants, mainly in the Miami neighborhood that is now called Little Havana.

In 1980 more than 100,000 people left Cuba for Florida during what became known as the Mariel boatlift. Most of these new immigrants were poor, and some were convicted criminals. Even Miami's established Cuban population had mixed feelings about the newcomers, particularly because the boatlift made some white Floridians more hostile toward all Hispanics. Upset about the influx of immigrants, irate south Florida voters tried to ban the use of the Spanish language in government activities by passing an English-only ordinance.

This energized Miami's Cuban community. Cuban exiles developed a Cuban-American economic and political presence in south Florida.

A brightly colored mural celebrating Cuban culture decorates the side of a building in Little Havana.

"We knew how to speak the language of the Venezuelans and Brazilians and the Argentineans in world trade," said Enrique Viciana, a Cuban-American accountant. "Miami became a market for Spanish speakers, even from Europe."

Today, a separate, largely Cuban-American editorial staff produces a Spanish-language edition of the *Miami Herald*. Cuban Americans, such as the Republican state senators Alex Diaz de la Portilla and J. Alex Villalobos, also play a significant role in Florida politics.

ASIAN AMERICANS IN FLORIDA

The Asian presence in Florida is growing in cities such as Tampa, where during the 2005 AsiaFest (a festival of food and music), the first Dragon Boat race was held. As of 2004 there were about 350,000 people of Asian descent living in Florida. The Asian-American population in Florida is not as significant as it is on the West Coast, in such states as California and Washington, but it is growing quickly. The number of Asian Americans living in Florida almost doubled during the decade between 1990 and 2000, and predictions are that this might happen again in the very near future.

Florida's Asian community takes in an Asian cultural event, the Hong Kong Dragon Boat Race, in Miami.

Asian Americans have not only become the fastest-growing minority group in Florida, they have made the Miami-Dade area a record holder. The Miami-Dade area is now the community with the fastest growing Asian-American population in the entire United States. Many of the Asian immigrants have come to Florida from Latin American countries, so they speak not only their native languages but also English and Spanish. This has helped them fit into Florida communities very easily. Many of the Asian immigrants are well educated and do well in business, such as Kiran Patel, who is of Asian-Indian descent, and his wife, Pallavi, who are both practicing physicians who made a large donation ($5 million) in 2002 to the Tampa Bay Performing Arts Center. In 2005 they also donated $18.5 million to the University of South Florida. Many other Asian Americans own dress shops or restaurants or are professionals, such as doctors, lawyers, and computer programmers. Almost half of all Asian immigrants living in Florida have college degrees and own homes. In other words the Asian-American community in Florida is thriving.

NATIVE AMERICANS IN FLORIDA

Although Native Americans were once the only inhabitants of the peninsula that makes up the present-day state of Florida, today the number of Native Americans living in the Sunshine State is low. The U.S. Census Bureau estimated that in 2004, fewer than 50,000 Native Americans made Florida their home. There are federally recognized Indian tribes living in the state. The Miccosukee Tribe has three reservations in the Miami area, and the Seminole Tribe of Florida has six, with its main headquarters in Hollywood. Members of the Muscogee Tribe, with a center in Bruce, and people of the Perdido Bay Tribe of the Lower Muscogee Creeks, in Pensacola, also live in the state.

Of the remaining tribes, the Seminole are the most prominent. With lands in Tampa, Brighton, Fort Pierce, Big Cypress, Immokalee, and Hollywood, the tribe keeps its traditions alive through performing ancient ceremonies and continuing the study of its languages. Otherwise, as one of the Seminole's Web sites states, these Native Americans live pretty much like everyone else, making trips to malls and grocery stores and an occasional call for a pizza delivery. Two of the tribes also have invested in the tourist trade by building gambling casinos on their reservations. Traditional arts and crafts as well as more modern forms of art are also sold.

Throughout the year Native Americans celebrate at gatherings called pow-wows. Dancers is full costume perform in traditional dances as the sound of drums fills the air. Native American foods and crafts are often sold at these gatherings, which are held annually at places such as Mount Dora and Vero Beach.

At the Miccosukee Tribe Arts Festival native crafts are on display for viewing and for sale.

WHO OWNS THE PAST?

Florida's various ethnic groups sometimes argue over how the state's troubled history should be presented. Although the Seminole Wars took place over a century ago, their heroes—on both sides—can still ignite passions today.

Every year since 1968, the Springtime Tallahassee Festival parade has been led by a man dressed like Andrew Jackson. Festival defenders maintain that this recognizes Jackson as an important person in Florida's development. But almost every year critics complain that this glorifies Jackson, whom they believe was viciously brutal to Native Americans and African Americans. "Blacks and Indians today can no more be expected to revere Andrew Jackson than Jews could be expected to revere Hitler," the Tallahassee journalist Roosevelt Wilson wrote during the 1993 springtime debate.

The symbol of Tallahassee's Florida State University (FSU) is the Seminole. FSU fans developed the "tomahawk chop," an up-and-down arm motion that Atlanta Braves baseball fans later picked up. Before every FSU home football game, a man depicting Osceola rides a horse into the center of the field and plants a burning spear. Florida's Seminole leaders have approved these practices, but Native American activists from other states have objected. "It's disgusting to the native people to see this trivializing of Indian culture," says the Indian activist Clyde Bellecourt.

POPULATION DENSITY

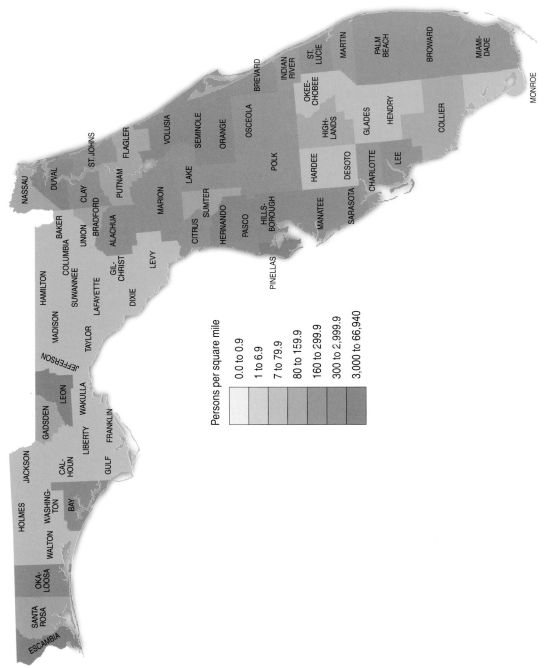

Persons per square mile

0.0 to 0.9
1 to 6.9
7 to 79.9
80 to 159.9
160 to 299.9
300 to 2,999.9
3,000 to 66,940

NASSAU
DUVAL
ST. JOHNS
FLAGLER
PUTNAM
CLAY
BRADFORD
BAKER
UNION
COLUMBIA
ALACHUA
GIL-CHRIST
LEVY
MARION
DIXIE
LAFAYETTE
SUWANNEE
HAMILTON
MADISON
TAYLOR
JEFFERSON
LEON
WAKULLA
GADSDEN
LIBERTY
FRANKLIN
GULF
CAL-HOUN
JACKSON
LIBERTY
WASHING-TON
BAY
HOLMES
WALTON
OKA-LOOSA
SANTA ROSA
ESCAMBIA
VOLUSIA
SEMINOLE
ORANGE
LAKE
SUMTER
CITRUS
HERNANDO
PASCO
HILLS-BOROUGH
PINELLAS
POLK
OSCEOLA
BREVARD
INDIAN RIVER
OKEE-CHOBEE
ST. LUCIE
MARTIN
PALM BEACH
BROWARD
MIAMI-DADE
MONROE
HIGH-LANDS
HARDEE
MANATEE
SARASOTA
DESOTO
CHARLOTTE
GLADES
HENDRY
LEE
COLLIER

COMING TOGETHER

Florida is not, nor has it ever been, a multicultural paradise. Conflicts have made the headlines from time to time. In spite of this, Florida's culturally diverse communities often mingle and get along.

Florida's bounty of cultural diversity allows everyone to experience and enjoy each other's differences.

One way people mingle with others from different cultures is during the variety of sports and entertainment events in which a lot Floridians invest their leisure time. In most of Florida, for instance, football is king. Come Friday night, many Floridians are generally in the stadium or glued to their television sets. Watching football is all the more tempting because Florida teams—high school, college, and professional—are so good. In recent years Florida's college teams have often vied for the nation's number-one ranking.

A popular sport in Florida that not many other states offer is jai alai (pronounced HIGH-LIE). Spaniards invented this game, and in Florida Cuban-American players dominate it. Often called the fastest and most dangerous sports game, jai alai (which means "merry festival") resembles a fast-paced combination of racquetball and badminton.

Cuban Americans are also well represented in baseball. Baseball teams—professional, collegiate, and Little League—find big audiences in every part of the state. In 2005 the Gators from the University of Florida were ranked second in the nation. And the Marlins' (one of Florida's professional baseball teams) Dontrelle Willis drew the crowds into the stadium in 2005, when he became the thirteenth African-American pitcher to win more than twenty games.

Many Floridians aren't content to sit in stadiums or in front of the television and watch sports. Golf courses and tennis courts blanket Florida, with many modern communities built around golf courses of their own. Because of Florida's warm weather, golfers and tennis players can play throughout the year, although thunderstorms can end games quickly.

No matter what ethnic background Floridians come from, common interests, such as raising families, working hard to make a good life, and enjoying the natural environment that the Sunshine State provides, can bring people together in spite of cultural differences.

THE CUBAN SANDWICH

There is no better way to forget cultural differences (or to enjoy them) than through sharing good food. Even Floridians who don't always appreciate the state's cultural diversity concede that it has produced a wonderful array of foods, ranging from Southern to Cuban, Mexican, Jewish, Chinese, and Indian. Restaurants offering authentic meals from these cultures are springing up in all sections of the state. Here is an ethnic food you can make for yourself at home. This is the best-known Cuban-American dish in Florida, although it is not actually from Cuba. In fact, turn-of-the-century Cuban-American cooks invented the "Cuban sandwich" in Tampa, and today the dish is popular throughout the state. Have an adult help you with this recipe.

- fresh Cuban bread
- Swiss cheese
- raw onions (optional)
- lettuce (optional)
- mustard
- sliced ham
- sliced roast pork
- pickles

Authentic Cuban bread is flat and circular, shaped somewhat like a flying saucer. If you can't find Cuban bread, French, Italian, or any light, fluffy bread will do.

Slice the bread in two the long way. Slice the cheese and shred the lettuce and onions, if you're using them. Spread mustard on the bread, and insert the meat, cheese, pickles, lettuce, and onions.

To complete the sandwich, you need to grill and press it. Because Cuban presses are hard to come by, you might use the flat, ungrooved side of a waffle iron, two iron skillets (one on each side of the sandwich), or even an iron. Once the sandwich has been flattened and the cheese is melted, enjoy.

Chapter Four

How Florida Works

The United States is governed by a document called the U.S. Constitution. Included in the U.S. Constitution is what is referred to as the Tenth Amendment, which declares that each of the states has certain rights and powers, as long as they do not conflict with the rights and powers of the federal government. For instance, none of the states is allowed to have its own army, to coin its own money, to grant titles of nobility (such as "king" or "queen"), or to engage in war with another state or another country.

HISTORY OF FLORIDA'S CONSTITUTION

Each state, in order to make it clear how it will run its local government and make its individual state rules, has a constitution. Before being admitted to the Union, each state had to appoint representatives who were responsible for creating a state constitution that would set the foundation for these state laws. Florida's first constitution was written in 1838 at Port Saint Joe on the northern Gulf Coast.

Florida's State Capitol houses the executive and legislative offices. It towers behind the Old State Capitol.

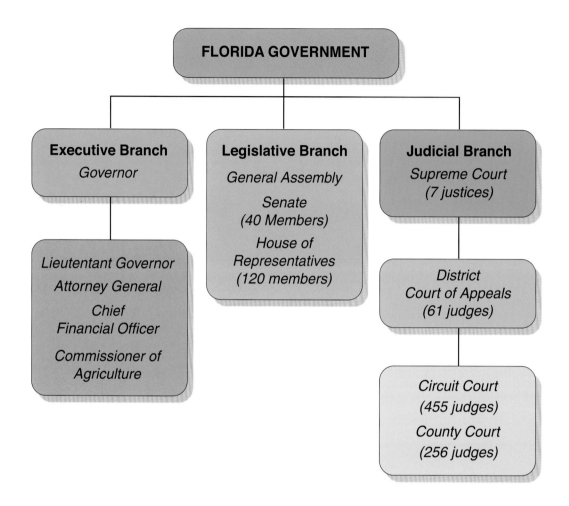

FLORIDA GOVERNMENT

Executive Branch
Governor

Lieutentant Governor
Attorney General
Chief
Financial Officer
Commissioner of
Agriculture

Legislative Branch
General Assembly
Senate
(40 Members)
House of
Representatives
(120 members)

Judicial Branch
Supreme Court
(7 justices)

District
Court of Appeals
(61 judges)

Circuit Court
(455 judges)
County Court
(256 judges)

Over the years parts of that original constitution became outdated. Amendments (or changes) can be written and added to the constitution, but sometimes an entirely new constitution is needed. For instance, in 1861, the constitution had to be changed when Florida ceded (or left) the Union prior to the Civil War. Then in 1865 another constitution had to be created to reflect that Florida was readmitted to the Union and that slavery in the state had been abolished. In 1868 the constitution was rewritten again.

This one gave the right to vote to all males in the state and provided seats for Seminoles in congress. Over the years Florida's constitution has been rewritten six times. The state constitution that is currently in use was created in 1968.

INSIDE GOVERNMENT

Florida's state government has three branches: executive, legislative, and judicial. In this way it resembles the federal government and other state governments. But the balance of power among the three branches is somewhat unusual in Florida.

Executive

The executive branch of Florida's state government administers and enforces laws. The governor serves as the head of this branch, along with three independently elected cabinet members. Florida is unique among the states in that the governor shares the responsibility and the power of this branch of government with the three members of the cabinet.

The governor is elected to a four-year term and may run for this position two terms in a row, along with his or her lieutenant governor. In 1968 the Florida state constitution was revised to include the position of lieutenant governor, whose main responsibility is to take over as the head of the state government should

Governor Jeb Bush, elected in 1998 and re-elected in 2002, strives for "limited government, the importance of education, and fiscal discipline" in governing the state.

something cause the position of governor to become vacant, such as the death or impeachment of the governor. The governor is the chief law enforcement officer of the state and appoints the heads of the many departments within the government, such as the department of education.

Members of the cabinet are elected to four-year terms and may run for office for as many terms as they want. The cabinet is made up of an attorney general, a chief financial officer, and a commissioner of agriculture. The attorney general is the main lawyer of the state; the chief financial officer is the main treasurer and comptroller of the state; and the commissioner of agriculture is in charge of programs that deal with Florida's farmers, food supply, and public lands, among other things.

Legislative

Florida's legislature passes laws and budgets and proposes changes to the state constitution. The legislature is composed of two chambers. The house of representatives has 120 members who serve two-year terms, while the senate has 40 members who serve four-year terms. Since 2000 legislators have only been able to serve for eight consecutive years.

Florida has one of the most powerful state legislatures in the country. Legislative leaders often ignore the governor's budget recommendations and come up with their own figures.

Judicial

Four levels of courts make up the state court system. County courts deal with misdemeanor charges and small lawsuits. The state's twenty circuit courts deal with felony charges and larger lawsuits. Judges serving in these courts are elected by Florida's voters.

Lower court decisions may be appealed to Florida's district courts of appeal and then to the Florida Supreme Court. The Florida Supreme Court reviews all death-penalty decisions. Cases involving

Florida's legislature meets to amend the state's constitution and to review laws and state budgets.

state or federal constitutional questions may go directly to this high court. Judges on these higher courts are appointed by the governor. But a governor cannot just appoint whomever he or she wants. Instead, the governor must choose from a list of from three to six names supplied by the Judicial Nominating Committee.

In Florida the courts are generally the most liberal branch of state government. Over the years they have proven perfectly willing to declare the actions of the governor or legislature unconstitutional.

FLORIDA BY COUNTY

PROBLEM SOLVING IN EDUCATION

Because of the great increase in population, which promises to continue at its current, fast pace, Florida school officials have had their hands full trying to accommodate all the new students while meeting national education standards. This struggle can be seen in a number of different ways.

Because of the increasing pressure on the environment caused by the destruction of natural habitat, land is becoming more and more scarce. Because of the hurricane destruction of the past few years, the cost of construction materials is at an all-time high. So in response, Florida has been building fewer but bigger schools as opposed to building a lot of smaller schools.

As Florida's population increases, overcrowding in schools has become an issue for state educators.

In the 2006 Quality Counts study compiled by *Education Week* magazine, it was determined that in all of the fifty states, Florida has the largest schools in the country. Many of Florida's high schools, for instance, enroll more than three thousand students. Some high schools even have student populations topping four thousand. Educators have found that this can cause a sense of alienation among the students. Some students feel lost in the huge crowds they encounter each day at school. They feel like strangers among their fellow classmates, because they know so few people in the massive student population. This sense of feeling alone, some educators believe, can cause additional strains on a student, possibly even leading to his or her wanting to drop out of school. According to a report by the Manhattan Institute for Policy Research, in 1998 Florida was one of five states that had the highest dropout rates in the country.

The dropout figures had not changed much by 2006, at least not according to some research. And that is another problem. The results of research can give different answers, depending on how the information is gathered and interpreted. Florida's Department of Education had interpreted the information differently than private research groups have.

In an effort to decrease the high dropout rate in Florida's schools, the Florida legislature suggested a bill in 2006 that would make Florida the first state to require high school students to declare a major field of study, just as college students do. Some representatives in the state legislature are hoping that making high school students decide on a particular field of study (such as English or math or auto repair) might make them more interested in high school, better prepared for college and the working world, and less likely to drop out of school. Opponents of this bill are concerned, however, that choosing a major so early might put too much pressure on students. Some Florida high schools already allow students to choose a major, but this law, if passed, would make it a requirement.

The Florida legislature is working in another direction that might help decrease the number of high school dropouts. In 1997 a program was financed by the Florida legislature to develop an online education program. Thus, Florida Virtual School was created. At first this online program started out offering only high school courses, but today, courses for students from the sixth through twelfth grades are available through the Internet. Students living in Florida, in any other state, and, in fact, in countries outside of the United States can enroll in and graduate from this virtual school. Florida Virtual School is the nation's largest statewide public online school, with 150 certified teachers who offer a wide assortment of courses.

This student is one of thousands who have enrolled in the Florida Virtual School of computer-based classes.

Chapter Five

Making a Living

Florida's fertile soil and long days of sunshine make the state both a good place to grow food and a nice place to go for a vacation. Thus agriculture and tourism are the two main ingredients of Florida's economy.

FARMING

Agriculture has fueled much of Florida's economic development, beginning with its earliest years and continuing into the twenty-first century. Draining the Everglades uncovered some fantastically rich soil, permitting the development of sugarcane fields south of Lake Okeechobee. It also helped turn the area southwest of Miami into the winter vegetable capital of the country.

Today, Florida is the nation's top producer of sugarcane. The state tops California in the production of such fresh vegetables as tomatoes, corn, and beans and comes in second in the production of bell peppers. Beef and dairy also play an important role in Florida's economy.

When most people think of Florida agricultural products, they think about oranges and grapefruits. There is a good reason for this.

A Florida orange picker unloads his haul at one of Florida's many groves.

Florida produces 79 percent of the nation's citrus fruit. Grapefruit production in Florida is the largest in the world, and only Brazil produces more oranges than the Sunshine State. Most of these oranges are not directly eaten but rather are squeezed into juice.

These oranges await processing at a juicing plant in central Florida.

Citrus groves once dotted much of Florida. The sweet smell of the blossoms perfumed the air each spring. But citrus trees are easily damaged when the temperature dips below freezing for too many hours or too many consecutive days, and this is what happened to many of the citrus fields in the northern part of the state. Suburban development has also eliminated many citrus orchards. Today, most of Florida's citrus groves are concentrated in the south-central part of the state.

Even though citrus groves produce an important crop for Florida's economy, they come in second in the agricultural industry as far as how much money they make for the state. The nursery and greenhouse industry is ranked number one. It produces plants normally seen growing in gardens around much of the nation. It sells plants such as flowers, shrubs, and grass.

Hybrid orchids are cultivated and sold at this Homestead nursery.

The number-three income producers in the agricultural industry are the vegetables and melons that are grown in Florida. Other farm products include items such as milk, eggs, poultry, and beef. There is also a nice amount of money made in the horse business. In 2006 it was estimated that there were 350,000 horses in Florida. Many of these horses are Thoroughbreds that are raised to compete in national races. Ocala is often referred to as the horse capital of the world, having produced forty-one horses that have won national championships.

There are about 42,500 farms in Florida, each with its team of employees. Farmwork is not easy, especially when it comes to chopping sugarcane and picking fruit. Until the middle of the twentieth century, Florida farmworkers were generally African American or Mexican American. Today, most are recent immigrants from Haiti, Nicaragua, El Salvador, Guatemala, and Vietnam. They are very vulnerable to being mistreated, said the farmworker organizer Tirso Moreno, because "they don't know English, they don't know the laws, and they have no relatives here." These farmworkers often face long hours, low pay, on-the-job accidents, and possible illnesses from exposure to pesticides.

Florida's farms employ many immigrant workers eager for employment.

Another major problem the agriculture business is facing is what is referred to as the "dumping" of produce from one country into another. Florida's farmers have complained that vegetables and fruits grown in Mexico are being brought to U.S. markets at such low prices that Florida farmers cannot compete with them. These products are being sold for less than it costs Florida farmers to grow and harvest them. This means that the selling of Florida produce is threatened. If Florida farmers cannot sell their produce, they could go out of business. Some farmers have filed antidumping petitions against Mexico. However, the dispute is far from being resolved, as Mexican farmers, in turn, have argued that the United States also dumps products into Mexico. Lawmakers are working on the problem.

2004 GROSS STATE PRODUCT: $599 Million

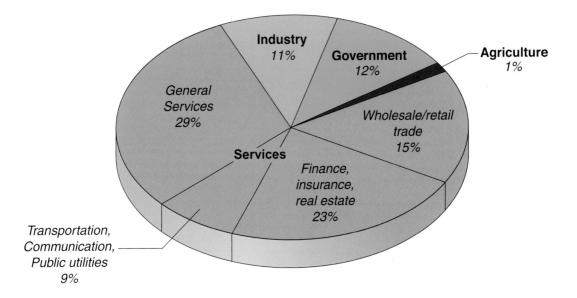

TOURISM

The same warm, sunny weather that helped make Florida an agricultural wonderland also attracted tourists to the state, eventually making tourism Florida's largest industry. Although Miami Beach was already a popular tourist destination in the 1950s, the Florida tourism economy did not go into high gear until the arrival of Walt Disney World outside of Orlando in 1971.

When Walt Disney and his brother, Roy, were looking for potential sites to build a new theme park complex, they considered Niagara Falls, St. Louis, and the Great Smoky Mountains. But none of these places could beat central Florida's great weather, open land, and cheap real estate. So the Disney brothers settled on a huge tract of wetlands and orange groves southwest of Orlando.

Some 35,000 people work at Walt Disney World, entertaining an estimated thirty million visitors a year. "We want our guests to feel that when they come onto the Walt Disney World property, they've left the real world behind, they've left behind their cares and worries, and they're here to have a good time," said Barbara Knapp, a Disney personnel manager. Walt Disney World helped to make central Florida one of the world's leading tourist destinations. However, today, Walt Disney World is just one part of Florida's large tourist industry.

The addition of Disney World has sparked central Florida's economic health by providing thousands of jobs. It was the most visited park in the world in 2005.

In 2005 more than 85 million people visited Florida. In that same year tourists brought $62 billion into Florida's economy. Where do many tourists spend their money when they go to Florida? They have to have someplace to sleep, so hotels receive a large portion of the money. Visitors to Florida also have to eat, so restaurants get some of it, too. After these expenses are paid, tourists generally want to have fun. Beaches and national parks, which charge entrance fees, are often packed with tourists. So are golf courses and tennis courts. However, many tourists head straight for the many interesting and often entertaining attractions. Some of the top attractions, besides Walt Disney World, include Universal Studios and Sea World in Orlando and Busch Gardens in Tampa. The Kennedy Space Center in Titusville and Cape Canaveral also gets its share of tourists eager to see a launch pad and to take a tour of the facilities.

One of Florida's most popular attractions is Universal Studios in Orlando.

FLORIDA WORKFORCE

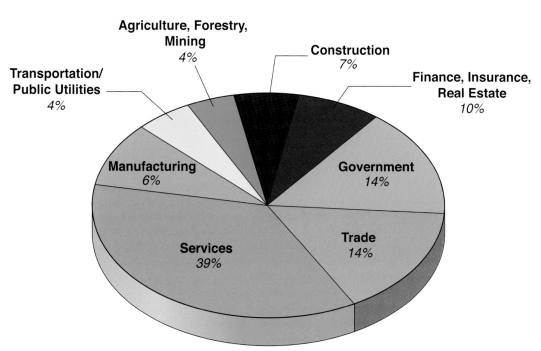

AIRPLANES AND ROCKETS

At the beginning of World War II, Floridians rallied around President Roosevelt's pleas for soldiers, with 250,000 people volunteering for service. That was a quarter of a million Floridians at a time when the total population of the state was only 1.8 million.

Another effect of the war on Florida was the building of military bases and training grounds for the soldiers who would be shipped overseas to fight. This military influence boosted Florida's economy, as the military built over 1,500 miles of highway, erected over forty aviation camps, and constructed massive military installations and housing to support over one million sailors, soldiers, and airmen who were stationed in the state.

In 1940 Florida was the least populated southern state. After the influx of the military and their families, however, the population began to grow. The word got out that Florida was a great place to live. The economy began to expand, too, as government defense contracts provid-ed jobs not just for the members of the military but also for businesses (such as shops, groceries stores, and construction companies) that serviced the military personnel.

In 1949 Cape Canaveral, on the Atlantic coast in central Florida, became the launching site for U.S. missiles, in part because of its good weather and seaside location. In 1962 Cape Canaveral, now known as the John F. Kennedy Space Center, was designated the Launch Operations Center. It is from Cape Canaveral and the Kennedy Space Center that all U.S. human space flights have been sent on their way to the moon and to the International Space Station. This program has had some tremendous successes.

The space shuttle Discovery *launches from the Kennedy Space Center.*

HISTORIC SPACE LAUNCHES

The U.S. space program has had many successes and some very sad disasters. People from all over the world, since the days of the first flights, have come to Florida's Kennedy Space Center to watch the huge rockets lift off the ground with a roar of fire from the engines and a loud cry of cheers from the audience.

One of the first important launches occurred on May 5, 1961, when Project Mercury's Alan B. Shepard Jr. became the first U.S. citizen to be launched into space. He was seated in *Freedom 7*, on top of a Redstone rocket, which reached an altitude of 116 miles above Earth. Basically, this was a quick ride up and down. The technology was not yet in place that could place a space capsule into orbit. When this ride was over, Shepard's space capsule landed 303 miles out into the Atlantic Ocean in what was called a splashdown. This first manned space flight lasted only 15 minutes and 28 seconds, but it would become a great historic event.

Project Mercury's capsules were only big enough for one person. It was not until the first flight of the Gemini Program in 1965, with Gus Grissom and John W. Young, that two people would enter space together. The Gemini Program paved the way for one of the most spectacular space flights, the one that would take a human to the moon (right). This distinction was given to the Apollo Program, a series of flights with capsules that were big enough to carry three people.

Unfortunately, the Apollo Program began with a disaster in 1967, when an intense fire broke out in the capsule as three astronauts waited for a launchpad test. But three years later after many safety adjustments were made, *Apollo 11* was launched. The day was July 16, 1969, and precisely on time at 9:32 a.m., with Neil Armstrong, Edwin "Buzz" Aldrin, and Michael Collins onboard, it lifted off the launchpad.

Millions of people all over the world watched this amazing event on their televisions. Four days later, on July 20, at 4:17 p.m., the lunar module touched down on what was called the Sea of Tranquility on the moon.

Many great events have followed, including the launch of space stations and the space shuttle *Columbia*, which also sometimes landed at the Kennedy Space Center. Florida residents as far away as Orlando know a few seconds before the shuttle will land because of the loud sonic boom that precedes the shuttle's arrival.

EARNING A LIVING

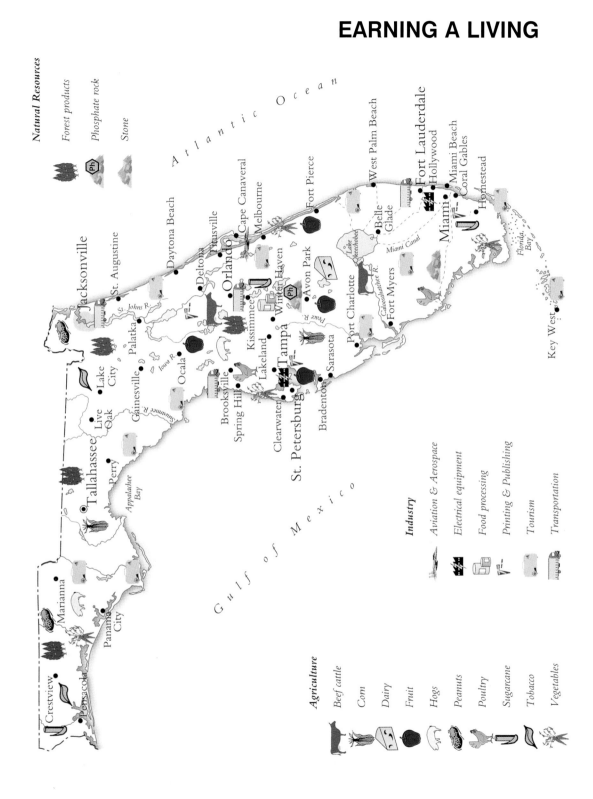

Natural Resources

Forest products

Phosphate rock

Stone

Industry

Aviation & Aerospace

Electrical equipment

Food processing

Printing & Publishing

Tourism

Transportation

Agriculture

Beef cattle

Corn

Dairy

Fruit

Hogs

Peanuts

Poultry

Sugarcane

Tobacco

Vegetables

Florida's warm weather and flat land have also encouraged the growth of the state's military industries, because they make ideal conditions for training pilots. Florida was awash with military training activity during World War II. A huge training facility called Camp Blanding was built in northeast Florida. Northwest Florida became the site of Eglin Air Force Base, the world's largest military base. Soldiers trained for the D-Day invasion of Europe during World War II on the Gulf beaches of the Big Bend's Camp Gordon Johnson. By the end of the war, forty military air bases were strewn throughout Florida.

In the following decades the American government's concern about possible conflicts with Cuba ensured that the military presence would continue to expand in Florida. Today, the U.S. Special Operations Command, headquartered in Tampa, directs major U.S. military operations. Even with budget cuts some 104,000 military personnel work in Florida, more than in all but five other states.

CHALLENGES TO BE FACED

Economic growth has both its good side and its bad side. During the last fifty years the state's expanding economy has fueled a rapid increase in Florida's population. This has caused some serious problems, such as the state's increasingly heavy traffic congestion and its high crime rate. These circumstances are making Florida a less attractive place for new residents and businesses. The problems have grown worse because Florida's state government has had trouble managing and coping with the growth.

Florida has a higher rate of deaths in car accidents than the national average. In Miami, drivers spend more time on the road than drivers in all but three other southern cities, and seven of the top twenty-eight most congested southern cities are in Florida.

Traffic congestion is an important issue that challenges Florida's state government.

The roots of these problems lie in the character of Florida's rapid development. Florida suffers from urban sprawl—the development of sparsely populated, far-flung suburbs. Urban sprawl lengthens drives between work, home, and shopping and discourages the development of mass transit.

A 1980s effort to require new residents and developers to build and pay for roads and public services *before* the need for them arose has fallen apart. As urban sprawl and poor planning continue, so do congestion and traffic accidents.

Another major problem is crime. Although Florida's crime rate has decreased over the past ten years, the state still ranks as one of the top five states in the number of crimes committed. In 2004 over 120,000 violent crimes were reported in Florida.

People don't agree on exactly what causes the state's crime problem. Some people stress the social problems that can contribute to crime. They point out that workers often earn low wages, and as a result, about one in five of Florida's children grows up in poverty. Florida's tax and welfare systems are also hard on some families, and Florida spends a relatively modest amount on schools. "They've cheated kids for a very long time in this state," said Mary Gonzalez, head of the Tampa area teachers' union.

Other people argue that Florida's crime problem is at least partially the result of a breakdown in families. They say that parents are not teaching their children morals, nor are they disciplining them.

Still other people believe that the state has been letting convicted criminals out of jail too easily. For many years, rather than spending money to build new prisons if the old ones were full, the state released convicts early. Many inmates out on parole committed more crimes.

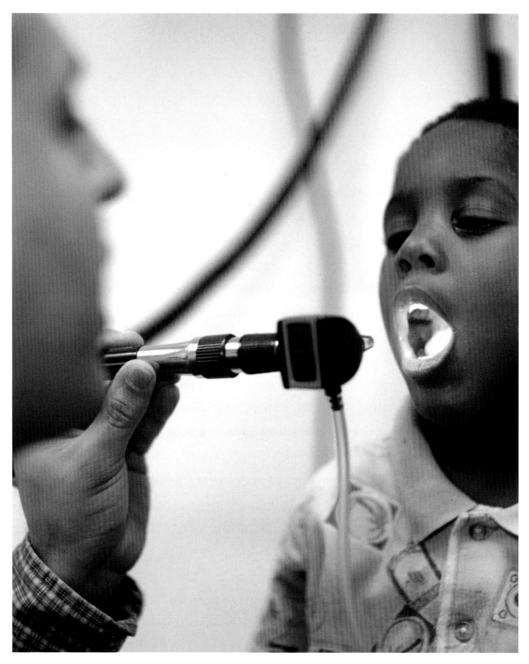

Some organizations provide free medical checkups for poor and homeless Florida residents.

The whole world heard about Florida's crime problem in the early 1990s. Twice in one year serial killers struck Gainesville, usually a quiet university town. Florida also suffered a rash of crimes against foreign tourists. Carjackings became a problem in Miami, and a British tourist sleeping at a north Florida rest area was killed during a botched robbery. The details of this murder underlined Florida's problem with troubled kids and easy probation: the apparent ringleader was a thirteen-year-old boy whom police had already arrested more than fifty times.

Faced with this highly publicized crime problem, Florida acted more aggressively than it had against congestion and environmental problems. The courts began sentencing teenagers convicted of crimes more strictly, and the state built more prisons, so adult convicts now spend most of their sentences in prison instead of out on parole. Florida also executes convicted killers at a higher rate than all but one other state.

Florida has also taken some steps to address the social problems that contribute to crime. It has improved access to health care for poor families with children and is experimenting with allowing community groups to run special public schools that students can choose to attend instead of regular public schools.

Florida will undoubtedly continue to face such problems as crime and congestion in the years to come. If these problems are allowed to fester, they could very well halt the growth that has transformed the state in the past half century. But most Floridians don't want that. They hope instead to find more creative ways to guide growth and reduce the problems that it sometimes causes.

Chapter Six

Touring the Peninsula

Spread across Florida's landscape is evidence of the state's diverse heritage. From the backwaters of northwest Florida to the coral reefs of the Florida Keys, the state is alive with nature, chock full of forts, and teeming with sites that lure tourists from all over the world.

THE BIG BEND

All around the Big Bend in Florida's panhandle is evidence of the state's Native-American and African-American past. Florida's largest Native-American mound site, the Lake Jackson Mounds, is located northwest of Tallahassee. These large earthen mounds, which were apparently used for ceremonial and possibly for burial purposes, were built by Native groups living in the area as long ago as 1000 C.E. Ironically, the seven grassy mounds sit next to a lake named for Andrew Jackson, who helped drive Native Americans from Florida.

Southwest of Tallahassee is Fort Gadsden Historical Site, site of the Negro Fort, where many African Americans and Native Americans

Visitors get a glimpse of eighteenth-century Saint Augustine as costumed women stroll past restored homes and shops.

were killed by Jackson's troops. The site offers a great view of the slow-moving Apalachicola River.

The Big Bend also features some of the state's most beautiful, pristine, and uncrowded beaches, such as Saint George Island, Saint Joseph Peninsula, and Saint Andrews. The boat rides at Wakulla Springs, one of the world's deepest and largest freshwater springs, offer a great look at the lush environment of inland north Florida. Visitors must beware of the alligators.

A family surf-fishes at Saint Joseph's Peninsula State Park.

NORTHEAST FLORIDA

In Saint Augustine, on the Atlantic coast, the historic Spanish Castillo de San Marcos still stands. Across the street is the old Spanish Quarter, where craftspeople work in buildings from the eighteenth century. Farther toward the center of town stand two opulent hotels built by Henry Flagler. One now houses a college, the other a museum that includes a magnificent collection of glasswork.

The beaches between Saint Augustine and Daytona Beach are among the few in the country that licensed motorists can drive on. The beaches are wide and made of hard, packed sand, which make them a great place to drive. Speed zones, entrance fees, and one-way routes help to direct the fun. The practice is controversial, for both environmental and safety reasons.

Vehicles are permitted to drive and to park on the beach in Daytona.

Early March brings Bike Week, when motorcyclists from around the country descend on Daytona Beach. In February stock-car racing enthusiasts crowd Daytona Beach to watch the Daytona 500.

Inland, in northwest Gainesville, is Devil's Millhopper, a deep sinkhole. A long staircase enables visitors to descend far into the hole.

TEN LARGEST CITIES

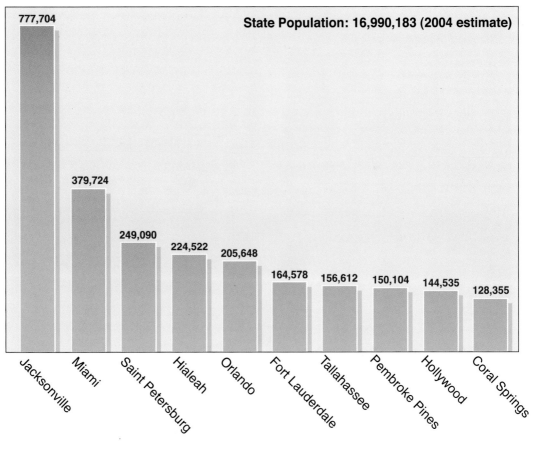

State Population: 16,990,183 (2004 estimate)

Jacksonville	777,704
Miami	379,724
Saint Petersburg	249,090
Hialeah	224,522
Orlando	205,648
Fort Lauderdale	164,578
Tallahassee	156,612
Pembroke Pines	150,104
Hollywood	144,535
Coral Springs	128,355

TAMPA BAY AND SOUTHWEST FLORIDA

Tampa showcases its multicultural heritage in the Ybor City district. A small museum illustrates the history of the area's cigar-making economy and immigrant culture. The other Ybor City highlight is the Columbia restaurant, perhaps the state's best-known eating establishment, which has been operating for more than one hundred years. In a covered courtyard visitors enjoy dining on the restaurant's specialty, paella (pie-AY-yah), a mixture of yellow rice, chicken, and seafood.

Across the Hillsborough River lies the Henry B. Plant Museum in the old Tampa Bay Hotel, complete with minarets. The hotel is now part of the University of Tampa. Another tourist destination is Busch Gardens, an amusement park in which monorails carry visitors around a park filled with African wildlife.

Tampa comes alive each year during two big events. In January the Gasparilla Pirate Fest begins with a mock invasion of the city by men masquerading as the legendary José Gaspar and his band of pirates. They sail into Tampa, land, and parade through downtown. During February northeastern Tampa is the site of the Florida State Fair, a two-week extravaganza complete with rides, rodeos, livestock and horse shows, and nightly concerts.

Men dress as pirates in a Tampa boat parade during the Gasparilla Pirate Festival.

Across the wide Tampa Bay is Saint Petersburg. The highlight of Saint Petersburg's waterfront is the Salvador Dali Museum. The museum features the world's largest collection of the Spanish surrealist's bizarre paintings and sculpture, including some gargantuan oil masterpieces.

South of Tampa Bay is Sarasota, long the headquarters of the Ringling Brothers and Barnum & Bailey Circus—the "Greatest Show on Earth." The circus tycoon John Ringling made his home there. A complex of buildings off Sarasota Bay pays homage to the Ringling family and the circus. The complex includes a wonderful circus memorabilia museum, an art museum that houses European paintings collected by the Ringling family, and the Ringling mansion.

Farther south, on the Gulf Coast near Fort Myers, are Sanibel and Captiva islands, which have some of the best seashell-hunting grounds in the state.

Sanibel Island is a seashell collector's dream.

ORLANDO AND THE SPACE COAST

Orlando is Florida's biggest tourist area. Walt Disney World officials are in the process of adding new attractions and revamping the Magic Kingdom. Increasingly, the park features not only classic Disney cartoon characters, such as Mickey Mouse and Donald Duck, but also characters from Disney's animated musicals, such as *The Little Mermaid*'s Ariel and *The Lion King*'s Simba. New attractions include Disney-MGM Studios and Animal Kingdom. Some Floridians never tire of Walt Disney World. Mary Eichin, who grew up near Orlando, says she has been to Walt Disney World roughly thirty times.

Another fun Orlando site is Universal Studios, where the rides and attractions are all based on movies. You can hop on a bicycle for a ride through the air with E.T., learn how fake earthquakes are made on movie sets, or watch makeup artists create gory monsters.

The only central Florida attraction that rivals Walt Disney World in size and originality is the Kennedy Space Center Visitor Complex. New, high-tech programs and IMAX movies bring the far reaches of space much closer. But a simple bus ride past the launchpads and the gigantic Vehicle Assembly Building, where technicians put together the space shuttles, can be equally satisfying.

Universal Studio's Islands of Adventure is a popular destination with teens.

PLACES TO SEE

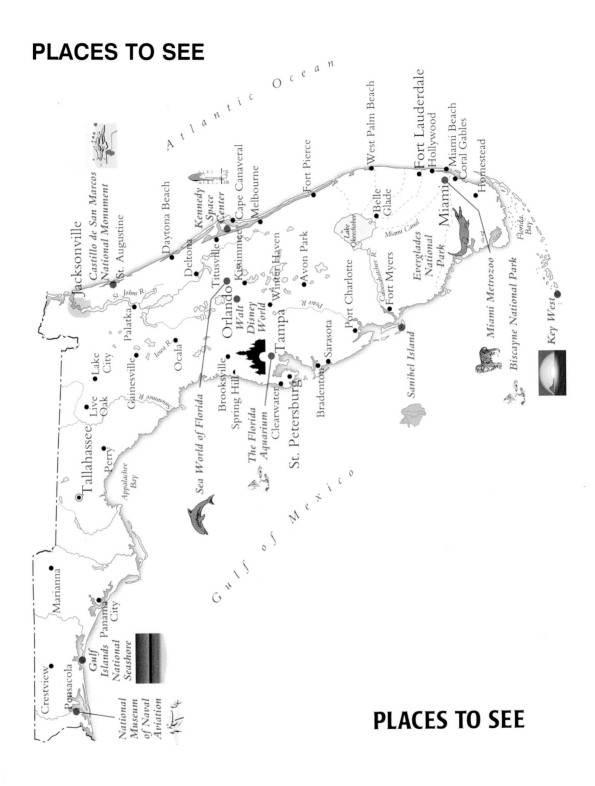

Atlantic Ocean

Jacksonville
Castillo de San Marcos National Monument
St. Augustine
St. Johns R.
Palatka
Iowa R.
Ocala
Gainesville
Lake City
Live Oak
Suwannee R.
Perry
Appalachee Bay
Tallahassee
Marianna
Crestview
Pensacola
Gulf Islands National Seashore
Panama City
National Museum of Naval Aviation

Daytona Beach
Deltona
Titusville
Kennedy Space Center
Cape Canaveral
Melbourne
Fort Pierce
Orlando
Walt Disney World
Kissimmee
Winter Haven
Avon Park
Sea World of Florida
Brooksville
Spring Hill
The Florida Aquarium
Tampa
Clearwater
St. Petersburg
Bradenton
Sarasota
Port Charlotte
Peace R.
Fort Myers
Caloosahatchee R.
Sanibel Island

Lake Okeechobee
Miami Canal
Belle Glade
Everglades National Park
West Palm Beach
Fort Lauderdale
Hollywood
Miami Beach
Coral Gables
Miami
Homestead
Florida Bay
Miami Metrozoo
Biscayne National Park
Key West

Gulf of Mexico

PLACES TO SEE

SOUTH-CENTRAL FLORIDA

Less well known but just as interesting is the interior of the southern half of the peninsula. There, farmworkers, wayward tourists, poorer retirees, and Native Americans share a less densely populated area of orange groves, sugarcane fields, phosphate strip mines, and wide prairies.

Although most of the state's orange groves are now farther south, the Florida Citrus Tower still rises above Clermont. Visitors can ride an elevator up the tower for the magnificent view. In tiny Mulberry, south of Lakeland, the curious Mulberry Phosphate Museum illustrates changes in the state's only major mining industry. Off the highway between Orlando and Titusville, the Fort Christmas Museum chronicles the Second Seminole War as well as the life of central Florida's poor rural families and the rise of the area's cattle-ranching industry.

South of Lake Okeechobee stretch the northern Everglades. Easily the most interesting stop in Everglades National Park is Shark Valley. Like most outdoor south Florida locales, this is an attraction that people should visit only in the winter months. During the summer the heat and mosquitoes are much too oppressive. At Shark Valley visitors can walk, bicycle, or take a two-hour tram ride into the Everglades along the trail, which ends at a tall observation deck that overlooks a huge saw grass marsh.

Visitors to Shark Valley can walk, take a tram, or bike along Tram Road to the observation tower.

Besides the stupendous view of the Everglades from the tower, Shark Valley's big draw is its alligators. Hundreds of alligators crowd the ponds around the observation tower. On the trail mother and baby alligators may sprint in front of visitor's bicycles.

MIAMI AND THE GOLD COAST

Both the Tamiami Trail and Interstate 75, dubbed Alligator Alley, lead east into Florida's largest metropolitan area, Miami–Fort Lauderdale–West Palm Beach. Extending west out of downtown Miami is Calle Ocho, "Eighth Street" in Spanish. The street is the center of the Little Havana neighborhood, where a McDonald's with Spanish-language signs is just one of the symbols of the Latin American presence in Miami.

Another symbol of Miami's Cuban-American population is the old *Miami News* building, dubbed the Freedom Tower. In the 1960s and 1970s, U.S. authorities turned this building into Miami's version of Ellis Island. There they processed thousands of Cuban exiles entering the country.

Across Biscayne Bay is Miami Beach. There South Beach's sultry nightclubs and pastel art deco buildings line Ocean Drive. Art deco was a style popular in the 1920s and 1930s that used bold, streamlined designs. Miami architects put their own local spin on the style, depicting palm trees and flamingos in the buildings' intricate designs. South Beach's eight hundred art deco buildings make up the largest collection of it anywhere. Walking through the chic neighborhood admiring the exuberant buildings, visitors also might see models and movie stars, because South Beach is a popular spot among the fashionable set.

The Berkeley Shore Hotel in South Beach displays the art deco architecture of the area.

FLORIDA FOLK FESTIVAL AND CALLE OCHO

They take place on opposite ends of the Florida peninsula, on opposite ends of the spring season. Even though both are celebrations of Florida's multicultural diversity, they seem like opposite extremes. One takes place amid the bright lights and noisy hubbub of a tropical city lined with sky-scrapers. The other takes place in the shade of oaks and Spanish moss along a slow, winding river on the outskirts of a sleepy Old South town. They are Florida's two most noteworthy annual festivals: the Florida Folk Festival and Calle Ocho (below), a part of the larger Carnaval Miami.

Each March the Miami event showcases south Florida's Latin her-itage. It started in 1978 as a fifteen-block open-house party on Eighth Street, Calle Ocho, in the heart of Miami's Little Havana. That year the event drew 100,000 people. Ten years later it drew one million. Advertised as the world's largest block party, the festival features the food, music, dance, and folk art of countries from around the Americas.

Seven hours north of Miami is White Springs, the tiny resort town that hosts the Florida Folk Festival.

Billed as one of the nation's oldest official state folk festivals, the three-day event showcases story-telling and fiddling from Florida's rural white culture and also features traditions from African-American, Native-American, and Latin-American cultures. During one weekend each May, 20,000 people stroll the festi-val's lush grounds, enjoying dance, music, and arts and crafts demonstrations.

THE EVERGLADES AND THE KEYS

The roads leading southwest out of Miami travel directly through the winter vegetable fields into Everglades National Park. In the winter the park is a bird-lover's paradise, as migratory fowl from all over North America spend the season there. At Flamingo, at the tip of the park, camping and canoe rentals are available.

It's also possible to camp across the bay on Key Largo, the first major key. Key Largo sits on the edge of one of Florida's major coral reefs. From John Pennekamp Coral Reef State Park, visitors can see the reef by snorkeling or taking rides on glass-bottomed boats. Visitors prone to seasickness should think twice about taking the boat rides. The authorities are actually trying to curb boat traffic around the reefs, so visitors with sensitive stomachs can tell their friends they're not queasy—they're just trying to save the environment.

The John Penneckamp Coral Reef State Park, established in 1963, is the first underwater park created in the United States. Here, boats are moored above the reefs.

THE FLAG: The Florida state flag, adopted in 1899, depicts the state seal on a field of white. Four red bars extend out from the seal to the corners of the flag.

THE SEAL: The state seal shows the sun's rays shining over a coastal scene, which includes a Seminole woman spreading flowers, a Sabal palmetto tree, and a steamboat on the water. Above the scene are the words "Great Seal of the State of Florida." Below the scene is the state motto, "In God We Trust." In use since 1868, the seal was officially adopted in 1985 after changes were made to the original.

State Survey

Statehood: March 3, 1845

Origin of Name: Florida was named by the
Spanish explorer Juan Ponce de León in April
1513. He may have chosen the name because
he arrived in the area during the Easter celebration, known as *Pascua Florida*, or "feast of
the flowers" in Spanish. Or he may have
named the land "Florida" because of the
many flowers he saw there.

Orange blossom

Nickname: Sunshine State

Capital: Tallahassee

Motto: In God We Trust

Flower: Orange blossom

Tree: Sabal palmetto palm

Bird: Mockingbird

Fish: Largemouth bass (freshwater);
Atlantic sailfish (saltwater)

Insect: Zebra longwing butterfly

Mockingbird

OLD FOLKS AT HOME

Stephen Foster wrote "Old Folks at Home" in 1851. He was living in New York at the time and had never visited the South when he wrote the song. His nostalgic view of the Old South strikes us today as somewhat out of date. "Old Folks at Home" became Florida's official state song in 1935, but currently there is a growing movement to find a more up-to-date song to represent the state.

by Stephen Collins Foster

Way down up - on the Swan - ee Ri - ver, Far, far a - way,
All up and down the whole cre - a - tion, Sad - ly I roam,

There's where my heart is turn - ing ev - er, There's where the old folks stay.
Still long - ing for the old plan - ta - tion, And for the old folks at home.

Chorus

All the world is sad and drea - ry, Ev - 'ry - where I roam.

Oh! dark - eys, how my heart grows wear - y, Far from the old folks at home.
(Lord - y,)

All roun' the little farm I wandered,
When I was young;
Then many happy days I squandered,
Many the songs I sung.
When I was playing with my brother,
Happy was I;
Oh! Take me to my kind old mother,
There let me live and die.

Chorus

Ole little hut among the bushes,
One that I love,
Still sadly to my mem'ry rushes,
No matter where I rove.
When will I see the bees a-humming
All roun' the comb?
When will I hear the banjo strumming,
Down in my good old home?

Chorus

Mammal: Florida panther

Marine Mammal: Manatee

Saltwater Mammal: Dolphin

Reptile: Alligator

Stone: Agatized coral

Gem: Moonstone

Shell: Horse conch

Soil: Myakka fine sand

Florida Panther

GEOGRAPHY

Highest Point: 345 feet above sea level, near Lakewood in Walton County

Lowest Point: Sea level along the coasts

Area: 58,560 square miles

Greatest Distance North to South: 450 miles

Greatest Distance East to West: 465 miles

Bordering States: Alabama to the north and west; Georgia to the north

Hottest Recorded Temperature: 109 °F at Monticello on June 29, 1931

Coldest Recorded Temperature: –2 °F at Tallahassee on February 13, 1899

Average Annual Precipitation: 54 inches

Major Rivers: Apalachicola, Aucilla, Blackwater, Caloosahatchee, Choctawhatchee, Escambia, Hillsboro, Kissimmee, Ochlockonee, Peace, Perdido, Saint Johns, Saint Marys, Suwannee, Withlacoochee

Major Lakes: Apopka, Blue Cypress, Crescent, George, Harney, Harris, Iamonia, Istokpoga, Kissimmee, Monroe, Okeechobee, Orange, Talquin, Tohopekaliga

Trees: Bahama lysiloma, bald cypress, black tupelo, custard apple, Florida fiddlewood, gumbo-limbo, laurel oak, live oak, longleaf pine, red mangrove, red maple, Sabal palmetto palm, slash pine, southern bayberry, southern red cedar, strangler fig, sweet bay, water hickory

Wild Plants: azalea, bougainvillea, bromeliad, cactus, camellia, coreopsis, dogwood, gardenia, golden begonia, hibiscus, iris, lupine, magnolia, mallow, marsh pink, oleander, orchid, pitcher plant, red bud, spider lily, sunflower, wood lily

Animals: black bear, dolphin, Florida panther, gray fox, Key deer, manatee, mangrove fox squirrel, marsh rabbit, opossum

Birds: anhinga, bald eagle, black-bellied tree duck, bobwhite quail, great blue heron, great egret, ibis, mangrove cuckoo, osprey, pelican, pileated woodpecker, reddish egret, redheaded woodpecker, red-winged blackbird, robin, roseate spoonbill, white-crowned pigeon, wild turkey, wood stork

Roseate spoonbill

Fish: bluefish, bluegill, catfish, chub, crappie, Chipola bass, Florida large-mouth bass, grouper, killfish, mackerel, marlin, menhaden, pompano, red snapper, sailfish, sea trout, striped bass, Suwannee bass, tarpon

Endangered Animals: American crocodile, Anastasia Island beach mouse, Cape Sable seaside sparrow, Caribbean monk seal, Choctawhatchee beachmouse, Everglades snail kite, finback whale, Florida grasshopper sparrow, Florida mastiff bat, Florida panther, Florida salt marsh vole, gray bat, Gulf moccasinshell, hawksbill sea turtle, humpback whale, Kemp's ridley sea turtle, Key deer, Key Largo cotton mouse, Key Largo woodrat, leatherback sea turtle, Lower Keys marsh rabbit, Ochlockonee moccasinshell, Okaloosa darter, oval pigtoe, Perdido Key beachmouse, red-coated woodpecker, rice rat, right whale, Saint Andrew beachmouse, Schaus' swallowtail butterfly, shortnose sturgeon, West Indian manatee, wood stork

Key deer

Endangered Plants: American caffseed, Avon Park harebells, beach jacquemontia, beautiful pawpaw, Britton's bear grass, Brooksville bellflower, Chapman rhododendron, Cooley's water willow, Florida golden aster, Florida torreya, Florida ziziphus, four-petal pawpaw, fragrant prickly-apple, Harper's beauty, Highlands scrub hypericum, Key tree-cactus, pygmy fringe tree, Rugel's pawpaw, scrub blazing star, scrub lupine, scrub mint, scrub plum, snakeroot, tiny polygala, wireweed

TIMELINE

Early 1500s The Calusa, Tequesta, Jeaga, Ais, Timucua, Apalachee, Tocobaga, and Alachua live in what is present-day Florida.

1513 Spanish explorer Juan Ponce de León claims Florida for Spain.

1565 Pedro Menéndez de Avilés of Spain founds Saint Augustine, the first permanent European settlement in what would become the United States.

1704 English forces attack Florida, destroying Spanish missions in the north and burning most of Saint Augustine.

1750 Creek Indians leave Georgia and settle in Florida, where they are joined by ex-slaves and members of other Florida tribes, becoming known as the Seminoles.

1763 Spain gives Florida to Great Britain in exchange for Cuba, which had been captured by the British in the Seven Years' War.

1783 At the end of the American Revolution, Great Britain returns Florida to Spain.

1817 First Seminole War begins when Seminoles attack a boat carrying American soldiers on the Apalachicola River.

1818 Andrew Jackson invades Florida, capturing Native-American villages and Spanish towns.

1821 Florida becomes part of the United States when Spain gives up its claim to the area.

1824 Tallahassee becomes the permanent capital of Florida.

1837 Seminole leader Osceola is captured by the Americans.

1842 Second Seminole War ends; many Seminoles are sent west; others move deep into the Everglades.

1845 Florida becomes the twenty-seventh state.

1851 East Florida Seminary opens at Ocala to train teachers; the University of Florida develops from this school.

1858 The Third Seminole War ends; fewer than two hundred Seminoles remain in Florida.

1861–1865 About 15,000 Floridians serve in the Confederate army during the Civil War.

1868 Florida adopts a new constitution that allows blacks to vote, and is readmitted to the Union.

1896 Henry Morrison Flagler's railroad reaches Miami from the north, opening up south Florida to development.

1925 Around 2.5 million people pour into Florida during the state's largest land boom.

1947 Everglades National Park opens.

1950 The army launches the first missile from the Long Range Proving Ground at Cape Canaveral.

1961 Alan Shepard takes off in a rocket launched from Cape Canaveral, becoming the first American in space.

1964 Dr. Martin Luther King Jr. leads demonstrations demanding equal rights for African Americans in Saint Augustine.

1969 *Apollo 11* astronauts land on the moon.

1980 Around 125,000 Cuban refugees come to Florida during the Mariel boatlift.

1986 The space shuttle *Challenger* explodes after takeoff at Cape Canaveral, killing all seven crew members.

1992 Hurricane Andrew, one of the greatest natural disasters in U.S. history, strikes south Florida; damages are estimated at $30 billion.

2000 All eyes are on Florida as the United States waits to find out if George W. Bush or Al Gore has won the state and, thus, the presidential election.

2005 A record-breaking year for hurricanes occurs, as twenty-seven named storms make an appearance, with four of them making landfall and causing damage in Florida.

ECONOMY

Agricultural Products: avocados, carrots, cattle, celery, cucumbers, eggs, grapefruit, hay, hogs, horses, lettuce, limes, oranges, peanuts, peppers, potatoes, poultry, soybeans, strawberries, sugarcane, sweet corn, tangerines, tobacco, tomatoes, watermelons

Manufactured Products: aviation and aerospace equipment, chemicals, cement, communications equipment, electrical equipment, medical instruments, processed foods, wood products

Natural Resources: clay, crushed stone, lime, lumber, peat, phosphate, staurolite, zircon

Business and Trade: communications, finance, printing and publishing, real estate, tourism, transportation, wholesale and retail trade

CALENDAR OF CELEBRATIONS

Olustee Battle Festival and Olustee Battle Re-enactment More than two thousand costumed actors take part in the mock fighting as they re-enact the battle that saved Florida from Union soldiers during the Civil War. Held at Lake City in February, the festival also includes a parade and the sale of arts and crafts.

Florida State Fair Tampa is home to this February celebration of Florida's best. You can see arts and crafts and Florida farm animals, enjoy the carnival rides, and eat great fair food.

Oranges

Chasco Fiesta This March festival in New Port Richey celebrates the friendship between the Calusa Indians and Spanish colonists. It includes a Native-American pageant with costumes and dancing, arts and crafts, and sporting events.

Florida Strawberry Festival Plant City celebrates its claim as the winter strawberry capital with eleven days of fun in March. Some of country music's biggest stars perform, and you can enjoy plenty of strawberries and other good food.

Strawberry Festival

Florida Heritage Festival This April festival in Bradenton celebrates the local area's history. The festival's highlight is the re-enactment of Hernando de Soto's 1539 landing at the mouth of the Manatee River.

Fiesta of the Five Flags This festival celebrates Florida's history under the flags of Spain, France, Great Britain, the Confederacy, and the United States. The landing of a Spanish explorer is re-created, and ceremonies mark the raising and lowering of the flags of the different countries. Sand sculpting and a treasure hunt are also part of this June festival in Pensacola.

Billy Bowlegs Pirate Festival Pirates invade the Fort Walton Beach Landing area during this June festival. About 1,500 ships crowd the harbor in honor of the local pirate legend Billy Bowlegs.

Tampa Bay Caribbean Carnival This carnival is held in June in Saint Petersburg. There is a costume parade; calypso, reggae, and salsa music; marching bands; arts and crafts; and plenty of food.

Possum Festival and Fun Day Not many Florida festivals feature main dishes of baked possum and possum hash, but this one does. This August festival in Wausau also serves up food other than possum, as well as live music and a parade.

Hispanic Heritage Festival This month-long Miami festival celebrates Spanish and Latin American culture. Hispanic folklore, arts and crafts, music, and foods are all part of the fun during this October event.

Florida Seafood Festival The state's oldest and largest seafood festival is held in Apalachicola every November. Oysters, crabs, and shrimp are the specialties here. For fun, try the oyster-shucking and net-throwing contests or watch the crab races.

American Sandsculpting Championship Festival At this November festival in Fort Myers Beach, you can watch professionals build the best sand castles around and join in the fun yourself.

Winterfest Boat Parade Fort Lauderdale is home to this December event that features one hundred decorated boats.

STATE STARS

Mary McLeod Bethune (1875–1955), originally from South Carolina, became famous for her educational efforts in Florida. In 1904 she opened the Daytona Normal and Industrial Institute for African-American girls. In 1923 the school joined with the Cookman Institute for African-American men to become Bethune-Cookman College, where she served as president for many years. Bethune also went to Washington, D.C., to advise President Franklin Roosevelt on minority affairs.

Ray Charles (1930–2004), who was raised in Greenville, lost his sight by the age of seven. He began studying music at the Saint Augustine School for Deaf and Blind Children. He went on to become an extremely influential musician by mixing gospel, rhythm and blues, and jazz to come up with soul music. His many hits include "Georgia on My Mind," "Hit the Road, Jack," and "What'd I Say."

Ray Charles

Jacqueline Cochran (1910?–1980) of Pensacola was the first woman to be elected to the Aviation Hall of Fame. After learning to fly, she became famous as a racing pilot. She organized the Women's Airforce Service Pilots (WASP) during World War II and in 1953 became the first woman to fly faster than the speed of sound.

Walt Disney (1901–1966) brought his creative genius to Florida when he developed the Walt Disney World theme park in Lake Buena Vista. Disney was famous for his animated films featuring such characters as Mickey Mouse and Donald Duck. He also started the Disneyland theme park in Anaheim, California.

Hamilton Disston (1844–1896), a northern businessman, proved that Florida's wetlands could be drained and made into valuable agricultural land. In 1881 Disston bought four million acres of land in central Florida and dug canals to drain the area. The city of Kissimmee grew as a result.

Marjory Stoneman Douglas (1890–1998) wrote a number of books about Florida, including *The Everglades: River of Grass*, which has become a classic. Most famous for her environmental work, Douglas also fought for women's rights and racial justice.

Gloria Estefan (1957–   ) moved to Miami from Cuba when she was two years old. She began her musical career with the Miami Sound Machine, which had its first big hit, "Anything for You," in 1988. She went on to have a successful solo career. Following a bus accident in 1990 that left her seriously injured, Estefan has made an inspirational comeback.

Chris Evert (1954–   ), who was born in Fort Lauderdale, is considered one of the greatest women tennis players of all time. Evert was the first woman player to earn $1 million. She counts three Wimbledon and six U.S. Open titles among her many wins.

Mel Fisher (1922–1999) spent sixteen years looking for the underwater wreckage of a Spanish boat that had sunk in 1622. When he finally found it near Key West in 1985, he became the best-known treasure hunter in the world. The silver, gold, and gems he recovered are worth as much as $400 million. Much of the treasure is on display in the Mel Fisher Maritime Museum in Key West.

Jackie Gleason (1916–1987) was the star of two of the most popular shows on early television, *The Jackie Gleason Show* and *The Honeymooners*. Although born in Brooklyn, New York, Gleason filmed both of his shows in Miami.

John Gorrie (1803–1855), a doctor, was living in Apalachicola in 1844. To help cool his malaria patients who ran high fevers, he built the world's first refrigeration machine, which produced blocks of ice.

Ernest Hemingway (1899–1961), who did much of his writing in Key West, is considered one of America's greatest authors. While living in Key West, Hemingway wrote *The Green Hills of Africa*, *For Whom the Bell Tolls*, and *To Have and Have Not*.

Zora Neale Hurston

Zora Neale Hurston (1903–1960), an important African-American writer, was born in Eatonville. Hurston's writing often dealt with the culture and folklore of the poor blacks living in the South. Her works include the novel *Their Eyes Were Watching God*, the nonfiction study *Mules and Men*, and her autobiography *Dust Tracks on a Road*.

James Weldon Johnson (1871–1938) of Jacksonville helped found the National Association for the Advancement of Colored People (NAACP) and served as its secretary for a number of years. He wrote poetry, song lyrics, and novels, most notably *The Autobiography of an Ex-Colored Man*. Johnson was also a U.S. diplomat to Venezuela and Nicaragua.

Sidney Lanier (1842–1881) is considered the best southern poet of the late 1800s, thanks to such works as "Corn" and "The Marshes of Glynn." Although from Georgia, Lanier spent much time in Florida because of his poor health, and he wrote *Florida: Its Scenery, Climate, and History*, an early guidebook to the state.

Lue Gim Gong (1858–1925) was born in China. He moved to Massachusetts and then to Florida, where he developed a cold-resistant orange that is still grown there.

Osceola (1803?–1838) was a great Seminole leader who opposed the removal of his people from Florida. Osceola led the Seminoles during the Second Seminole War until he was captured. He later died while being held prisoner.

Osceola

Ruth Bryan Owen (1855–1954), the daughter of the politician William Jennings Bryan, moved to Miami to take a teaching position. Owen ran for the U.S. House of Representatives in 1928 and won, becoming the first woman from the Deep South to serve in Congress. She later became the first female U.S. diplomat, when she served as minister to Denmark.

John D. Pennekamp (1898–1978) was editor of the *Miami Herald*. His campaign to save the Everglades from overdevelopment led to the creation of Everglades National Park. John Pennekamp Coral Reef State Park, near Key Largo, is named in his honor.

A. Philip Randolph (1889–1979), who was born in Crescent City, helped organize the Brotherhood of Sleeping Car Porters union for African-American workers. Randolph was also a civil rights leader who led marches on Washington, D.C., in 1941 and 1963.

Majorie Kinnan Rawlings (1896–1953) began writing when she moved to Cross Creek. Her 1939 Pulitzer Prize-winning novel, *The Yearling*, is set in rural north Florida. Her book *Cross Creek* was made into a movie in 1983.

Janet Reno (1938–   ), a Miami native, was the first woman to serve as attorney general of the United States from 1993–2001. Previously, she had been state attorney for the Miami area from 1978–1993.

Wesley Snipes (1962–   ), one of America's leading African-American actors, was born in Orlando. He then spent several years in New York, but during his teens, he returned to Orlando, where he took up acting. Snipes has starred in such films as *Rising Sun, Blade, Hard Luck,* and *Chasing the Dragon.*

Mel Tillis (1932–   ), a country music great, grew up in Pahokee. Tillis's songs, such as "Ruby, Don't Take Your Love to Town," have been recorded by many artists, including Jimmy Dean, the Everly Brothers, and Tom Jones. His daughter, Pam Tillis, who is also a popular country music singer, was born in Plant City.

Tiger Woods (1975–   ), who calls Orlando home, is a golfing sensation. After turning professional at age twenty-one, Woods won the Masters Tournament on his first try as a pro. In 2005 Woods won his tenth major golf tournament. He and his wife, Elin, also own property on Jupiter Island.

Tiger Woods

Vincente Martinez Ybor (1818–1896) was a Cuban immigrant who made his fortune making cigars. Ybor set up his first cigar factory in Key West, then moved to the Tampa area. Ybor City, the Cuban community that grew up around the cigar factories, later became part of Tampa.

TOUR THE STATE

Bird Emergency Aid and Kare Sanctuary (B.E.A.K.S.) (Big Talbot Island)
At the sanctuary you can see how thousands of injured wild birds are cared for. Birds on view include eagles, pelicans, owls, and ospreys.

Castillo de San Marcos National Monument (Saint Augustine) This massive fort built of coquina (a limestone formed from little shells) by the Spanish in the late 1600s has walls 8 to 12 feet thick and 33 feet high. Inside, exhibits trace the history of the fort and Saint Augustine. You might even get to see one of the fort's old cannons fired.

Daytona International Speedway (Daytona Beach) Known as the world center of racing, the speedway hosts many races, such as the Daytona 500 stock car race. You can tour the racetrack, watch videos of early races, and look over stock cars and other racing artifacts.

Kennedy Space Center Visitor Complex (Titusville) The visitor center at this site features a moon rock, space vehicles, and many displays tracing the history of the U.S. space program. You can also take a bus tour that provides views of the launchpads where space shuttles take off.

Daytona International Speedway

Mulberry Phosphate Fossil Museum (Mulberry) At this museum you can view some of the dinosaur remains found in the area known as Bone Valley. Other exhibits focus on the history of phosphate mining.

Walt Disney World (Lake Buena Vista) Central Florida is home to the most popular vacation spot in the world. Walt Disney World is made up of four major theme parks, The Magic Kingdom, EPCOT Center, Disney-MGM Studios, and Disney's Animal Kingdom along with two water parks and a number of other attractions.

Universal Studios Florida (Orlando) Ever wonder how they create the scary makeup in horror movies or the great stunts in action movies? This is the place to find out. Shows and exhibits demonstrate how movies are made. Rides such as Shrek, Fear Factor Live, and Men in Black let you become part of some of your favorite movies and television shows.

Charles Hosmer Morse Museum of American Art (Winter Park) This museum features more than 4,000 works of American art. Pottery and paintings are on view, as are many beautiful stained-glass windows by the famed designer Louis Tiffany.

Butterfly World (Coconut Creek) Here you can watch thousands of butterflies fluttering in two-story screened enclosures, which resemble gardens and a rain forest. You can also visit a butterfly breeding laboratory and a display of rare butterflies and insects from around the world.

International Swimming Hall of Fame (Fort Lauderdale) The world's greatest swimmers, including Johnny Weissmuller, Esther Williams, and Mark Spitz, are showcased at this site. Olympic medals and trophies are on display, and an art gallery and videos help tell the story of competitive swimming.

Miami Metrozoo (Miami) At this zoo animals roam free in areas that look like their natural habitats. The Asian River Life exhibit contains leopards, monitors, and pythons. Rare Bengal white tigers can be seen in a display that resembles the ruins of an Asian temple. The zoo also has playgrounds, animal shows, and a petting zoo.

Biscayne National Park (Outside Miami) Ninety-five percent of this unusual national park is underwater. The park showcases a great variety of sea life, ranging from manatees to brightly colored parrot fish. Trips on glass-bottomed boats are the best way to see the park's beautiful coral formations and tropical fish.

Biscayne National Park

Everglades National Park (Homestead) This park is home to more than 40 species of mammals, more than 350 species of birds, and more than 50 reptile species, including the alligator. The Everglades has hiking trails, some with boardwalks, and trams from which you can view the wildlife.

Mel Fisher Maritime Museum (Key West) More than $40 million worth of treasure from old Spanish ships is on display at this museum. Gold, silver, emeralds, diamonds, brass cannons, and historic artifacts can be viewed. One gold chain is 12 feet long and weights more than 6 pounds.

Edison and Ford Winter Estates (Fort Myers) Friends Henry Ford and Thomas Edison spent their winters together at these mansions in Fort Myers. The Ford home displays antique cars. The Edison home contains the inventor's laboratory, where he worked on the lightbulb and phonograph while on "vacation." A collection of Edison's inventions, ranging from talking dolls to the world's first phonograph record, are also on display.

The Bailey-Matthews Shell Museum (Sanibel Island) This museum has the most comprehensive collection of shells in the country. The thousands of shells on display represent only one-third of all the types of shells in the world. The museum also contains interactive displays and shell art.

J. N. "Ding" Darling National Wildlife Refuge (Sanibel Island) Habitat for more than 220 types of birds, including roseate spoonbills and brown pelicans, this park is a bird-watcher's paradise. There are both walking and driving trails through the refuge.

The John and Mable Ringling Museum of Art (Sarasota) John Ringling of Ringling Brothers' Circus fame collected great works of European art, which are exhibited at this Sarasota home. Just as interesting as the art is the Circus Museum, located in another building on the grounds, which displays parade wagons, costumes, posters, photos, and other circus items.

Museum of Science and Industry (Tampa) This popular museum contains exhibits on everything from hurricanes to butterflies to the human body. You can experience hurricane-strength winds in the Gulf Coast Hurricane exhibit. Then you can hike 3 miles of Florida wilderness in the Back Woods exhibit. Much of the museum features hands-on displays, such as fossils you can touch.

Pioneer Florida Museum (Dade City) Explore what it was like for Florida's pioneers at this museum, which includes an old schoolhouse, church, home, and railroad station. The museum also displays early farm tools, carriages, and Native American items.

Stephen Foster State Folk Culture Center State Park (White Springs) Stephen Foster made the Suwannee River famous in his song "Old Folks at Home." Today, you can learn more about Foster and his songs on the banks of the Suwannee. You can also see exhibits on Florida folk arts, such as basket weaving, blacksmithing, and woodworking.

National Museum of Naval Aviation (Pensacola) The history of naval flight is the focus of this museum, where you can see famous navy fighter planes, such as the F-14 Tomcat, as well as models of aircraft carriers and early blimps. There are even hands-on displays that let you take the controls of navy training equipment.

FUN FACTS

The world's first scheduled commercial airplane flight was made in Florida in 1914. The seaplane, piloted by Tony Jannus, flew between Saint Petersburg and Tampa.

Jacksonville is the largest city in the United States in land area. The city covers some 840 square miles.

Scuba divers can spend a night underwater at Jules' Undersea Lodge near Key Largo. The two-room hotel, originally an undersea research laboratory, sits 30 feet below the ocean's surface and has large windows that allow guests to view life under the sea.

Florida has a bat hotel that has remained vacant for almost seventy years. Clyde Perky built the tower in 1929 on Sugarloaf Key to attract bats to eat the mosquitoes that were bothering guests at his fishing lodge. Perky even put bat droppings inside to encourage local bats to move in, but none ever did.

Florida has lots of sinkholes, places where the limestone roof of an underground cavern collapses, making a hole in the ground. The state's largest opened up in 1981 at Winter Park. It measured 300 feet across and 100 feet deep. One house, six cars, parts of two streets, and a swimming pool were swallowed up.

Florida has more thunderstorms than any other state. Fort Myers is the leading city for storms, with around one hundred days with lightning each year.

Find Out More

If you want to learn more about Florida, look for these titles at your local library or bookstore.

GENERAL STATE BOOKS

Knotts, Bob. *Florida History*. Portsmouth, NH: Heinemann, 2002.

SPECIAL INTEREST BOOKS

Carlson, Charlie. *Weird Florida*. New York: Sterling, 2005.

De Wire, Elinor. *Florida Lighthouses for Kids*. Sarasota: Pineapple Press, 2004.

Grunwald, Michael. *The Swamp: The Everglades, Florida, and the Politics of Paradise*. New York: Simon and Schuster, 2006.

Haehle, Robert G. *Native Florida Plants*. Boulder, CO: Taylor Trade Publishing, 2004.

Tekiela, Stan. *Birds of Florida Field Guide*. Cambridge, MN: Adventure Publications, 2005.

Smithsonian Handbooks: Birds of Florida. Washington, D.C.: DK Publishing, 2002.

Whitney, Ellie, et al. *Priceless Florida: Natural Ecosystems and Native Species*. Sarasota: Pineapple Press, 2004.

Florida Kids

www.flheritage.com/kids

This is the Office of Cultural and Historical Programs Web site just for kids. It includes information on Florida's culture and history.

Online Sunshine

www.leg.state.fl.us/kids/

The kid's page from the Web site of Florida's legislature abounds with fast facts, a tour of the capitol, information on the state legislature, games, puzzles, and more.

Florida

www.kidskonnect.com/Florida/FloridaHome.html

This site is dedicated to the state of Florida, showcasing the state symbols and providing links to many Florida-related sites.

Index

Page numbers in **boldface** are illustrations and charts.

ABOUT THE AUTHORS

Perry Chang grew up in Gainesville and Tallahassee and has traveled the state with family and friends. Chang has worked as a reporter for two north Florida newspapers, the *Panama City News-Herald* and *Florida Flambeau,* and for the Florida capital bureau of the United Press International. A specialist in the southern United States, he has published numerous articles about the history of Florida.

Joyce Hart, a published writer and professional editor, has enjoyed many years of living in the Orlando area. Her father was stationed at the local air force base there, and most of Hart's family still lives in central Florida. Hart loves the warm weather and the great beaches that Florida offers, but she missed the mountains she had once known, so she eventually moved to the Pacific Northwest. Her sisters often pretend to send her packages of sunshine now, because the Pacific Northwest has so many cloudy days.